# TRACING YOUR
# WEST COUNTRY
# ANCESTORS

# FAMILY HISTORY FROM PEN & SWORD BOOKS

*Birth, Marriage and Death Records*
David Annal and Audrey Collins

*Tracing Your Channel Islands Ancestors*
Marie-Louise Backhurst

*Tracing Your Yorkshire Ancestors*
Rachel Bellerby

*Tracing Your Royal Marine Ancestors*
Richard Brooks and Matthew Little

*Tracing Your Pauper Ancestors*
Robert Burlison

*Tracing Your Huguenot Ancestors*
Kathy Chater

*Tracing Your Labour Movement Ancestors*
Mark Crail

*Tracing Your Army Ancestors*
Simon Fowler

*A Guide to Military History on the Internet*
Simon Fowler

*Tracing Your Northern Ancestors*
Keith Gregson

*Tracing Your Ancestors Through Death Records*
Celia Heritage

*Your Irish Ancestors*
Ian Maxwell

*Tracing Your Scottish Ancestors*
Ian Maxwell

*Tracing Your London Ancestors*
Jonathan Oates

*Tracing Your Tank Ancestors*
Janice Tait and David Fletcher

*Tracing Your Air Force Ancestors*
Phil Tomaselli

*Tracing Your Secret Service Ancestors*
Phil Tomaselli

*Tracing Your Criminal Ancestors*
Stephen Wade

*Tracing Your Police Ancestors*
Stephen Wade

*Tracing Your Jewish Ancestors*
Rosemary Wenzerul

*Fishing and Fishermen*
Martin Wilcox

*Tracing Your Canal Ancestors*
Sue Wilkes

*Tracing Your Lancashire Ancestors*
Sue Wilkes

# TRACING YOUR WEST COUNTRY ANCESTORS

*A Guide for Family Historians*

## KIRSTY GRAY

*Happy Hunting*

*Kirsty Gray*

Pen & Sword
**FAMILY HISTORY**

First published in Great Britain in 2013 by
**PEN AND SWORD FAMILY HISTORY**
an imprint of
Pen & Sword Books Ltd
47 Church Street
Barnsley
South Yorkshire
S70 2AS

ISBN 978 1 84884 783 5

A CIP catalogue record for this book is
available from the British Library

Typeset in 10pt Palatino by Mac Style, Driffield, East Yorkshire
Printed and bound in the UK by CPI Group (UK) Ltd, Croydon, CR0 4YY

Pen & Sword Books Ltd incorporates the Imprints of Pen & Sword
Aviation, Pen & Sword Family History, Pen & Sword Maritime, Pen
& Sword Military, Pen & Sword Discovery, Wharncliffe Local History,
Wharncliffe True Crime, Wharncliffe Transport, Pen & Sword Select,
Pen & Sword Military Classics, Leo Cooper, The Praetorian Press,
Remember When, Seaforth Publishing and Frontline Publishing.

For a complete list of Pen & Sword titles please contact
PEN & SWORD BOOKS LIMITED
47 Church Street, Barnsley, South Yorkshire, S70 2AS, England
E-mail: enquiries@pen-and-sword.co.uk
Website: www.pen-and-sword.co.uk

# CONTENTS

# PREFACE

With its catchy title of *Tracing Your West Country Ancestors*, it is clear what forms the basis of this book, and those with forebears and research interests in the City of Bristol, Somerset, Devon and Cornwall will certainly benefit from having a copy on the shelf. A veritable doorstop of a book would not cover all aspects of the research into the history of the people of the West Country and this small offering will definitely not ensure that your doors remain ajar in any fashion. However, I live in hope that what this book will achieve is to provide you with solid foundations in a vast array of subject areas specific to the West Country, highlighting particular documents, websites, resources, record offices and hidden treasures available to enhance your knowledge of the life and times of your forebears and their communities, as well as how things have changed over the centuries.

All the images included are either from my own personal collection, graphically produced by me or taken from documents, indexes, transcripts and catalogues from local archives, unless otherwise stated. Having searched through these documents over the years, it will not be a great surprise that many images and references relate to my own family history and I anticipate that highlighting these characters, and providing a little window into their histories, will bring alive some of the subjects discussed.

There is no way on earth that this book could ever have been completed without the unstinting support of many genealogical colleagues, my parents and friends, and a special mention must be given to Sue Maunder, my mum, and Maureen Selley, Chairman of the Devon Family History Society, both of whom had the dubious pleasure of reading this book from cover to cover before the rest of the world could feast their eyes upon it.

From a small acorn of an idea, a tree has grown and I hope that all who decide to leaf through the branches of this particular tree will enjoy the content and learn something along the way.

*Chapter 1*

# INTRODUCTION
# TO THE REGION

The West Country is a term used to define the region of south-west England between the Bristol Channel and English Channel. As with any informal area, the boundaries are difficult to define precisely and as a consequence a number of different definitions are used. Some groups use the term as roughly synonymous with the south-west region, while others use it more specifically to refer to either the northern part of the region, or the south-western part. The term is also used, for example, to refer to sports matches between cities such as Bristol and Bath or Gloucester and Bath. This guide encompasses the counties of Cornwall, Devon and Somerset, along with the City of Bristol, when referring to the West Country.

The coastline, the moors, agricultural land and the mining industry form a significant part of the region's geography and affect almost every aspect of its history as it impacts upon the people residing in villages, their occupations and everyday lives. Separated from the mainstream of national life through poor transport systems in and out of the counties, the hardy residents of the West Country, isolated, lacking riches and wresting poor livings from the land or the mines, or netting the bounty from the sea, were ever outward-looking, questing and fiercely independent. Daring mariners established trading links as early as the Bronze Age with fellow Celts in Brittany, Wales and Ireland. Later, Roman trading ships beached in southern coves to load tin, a metal much in demand for coinage.

The counties have many physical features in common, with their geology and terrain greatly influencing their history. The heights and depths of cliff tops and deep valleys, medieval boroughs and market towns, remote villages and hamlets define the region, though each county has its own distinct identity, characteristics and stories to tell.

## 1.1 The City of Bristol

Archaeological finds believed to be 60,000 years old, discovered at Shirehampton and St Annes, provide 'evidence of human activity' in the Bristol area from the Palaeolithic era. There are Iron Age hillforts near the city at Leigh Woods and Clifton Down on the side of the Avon Gorge, and on Kingsweston Hill near Henbury. During the Roman era there was a settlement, *Abona*, at what is now Sea Mills, connected to Bath by a Roman road, and another at the present-day Inns Court. There were also isolated Roman villas and small Roman forts and settlements throughout the area.

The town of *Brycgstow* (Old English: 'the place at the bridge') appears to have been founded in around 1000, and by 1020 was an important enough trading centre to possess its own mint, producing silver pennies bearing the town's name. By 1067 the town was clearly a well fortified *burh* that proved capable of resisting an invasion force sent from Ireland by Harold's sons. Under Norman rule, the town acquired one of the strongest castles in southern England.

The area around the original junction of the River Frome with the River Avon, adjacent to the original Bristol Bridge and just outside the town walls, was where the port began to develop in the eleventh century. By the twelfth century Bristol was an important port, handling much of England's trade with Ireland, including slaves. In 1247 a new stone bridge was built, which was replaced by the current Bristol Bridge in the 1760s.

With a population of 428,200 individuals in the 2011 Census, Bristol is the sixth most populous city in England, as well as being a ceremonial county. Historically split between the counties of Gloucestershire and Somerset, the city received a royal charter in 1155 and was granted county status in 1373. Bristol is built around the River Avon and it has a short coastline on the Severn estuary, which flows into the Bristol Channel.

Bristol, in contrast to the other counties of the West Country, is densely populated, with over 3,600 inhabitants per square kilometre (9,400 per square mile) in 2011. It has more than 3,500 listed buildings, with Sir John Betjeman proclaiming that Bristol had 'the finest architectural history of any city outside London'. However, in many other facets Bristol does not have such a positive reputation, especially the eighteenth-century slave trade and the 1980 riots that signalled all the social problems that would later lead to the inner city unrest in Liverpool and Brixton. Bristol's literary image also follows a certain tradition: in Chapter 38 of The *Pickwick Papers*, Mr Winkle visits the city, which 'struck him as being a shade more dirty than any place he had ever seen'. Virginia Woolf saw it in 1935, found its horrors indescribable and called it 'the most hideous of all towns'.

## 1.2 Somerset

With the Bristol Channel on the west, Bristol and Gloucestershire to the north, Wiltshire to the east, Dorset to the south-east and Devon to the south and south-west, Somerset is oblong in shape, being approximately 130 kilometres (80 miles) in length and just 58 kilometres (36 miles) in breadth. The administrative town of Taunton is the largest town in the county, located in the south, near the border with Devon. With a population of 917,100 individuals in 2011, Somerset is more densely populated than the other West Country counties of Devon and Cornwall, with two cities and several large urban areas.

Somerset is a rural county of rolling hills, such as the Blackdown Hills, Mendip Hills, Quantock Hills and Exmoor National Park, and large flat expanses of land, including the Somerset Levels. There is evidence of human occupation from Palaeolithic times and extensive archaeological sites such as Cheddar Gorge, Gough's Cave and Aveline's Hole have been discovered, with the latter housing examples of cave art. Subsequent settlement occurred in the Roman and Anglo-Saxon periods with the county playing a significant part in the consolidation of power and rise of King Alfred the Great, and later in the English Civil War and the Monmouth Rebellion.

The county name derives from the Old English *Sumorsæte*, which is short for *Sumortūnsæte*, meaning 'the people living at or dependent upon Sumortūn'. The first known use of the name *Somersæte* was in 845, after the region fell to the Saxons. Somerton is the modern Sumortūn and may mean 'summer settlement' – a farmstead occupied during the summer but abandoned in the winter. However, Somerton is not down on the levels – lower ground, where only summer occupation was possible because of winter flooding – but on a hill, where winter occupation was feasible. An alternative suggestion is that the name derives from *Seo-mere-saetan*, meaning 'settlers by the sea lakes'.

The people of Somerset are first mentioned in the Anglo-Saxon Chronicle's entry for AD 845, in the inflected form 'Sumursætum', but the county is first mentioned in the entry for 1015 using the same name. The archaic county name 'Somersetshire' is first mentioned in the Chronicle's entry for 878.

## 1.3 Devon

Devon is often referred to as Devonshire, although the county has never been officially a 'shire'. It shares land borders with Cornwall to the west and Dorset and Somerset to the east, the southern coast with the English Channel and the northern coast with the Bristol Channel.

Uncommonly large and diverse, Devon is the third largest of the English counties by area and boasts two moors, Dartmoor and Exmoor, as well as two coasts. The north coast around Lynton, with its great granite rocks, is known as the 'English Switzerland'; the south coast, in contrast, has red sandstone cliffs, subtropical vegetation and deep estuaries. The biggest county in southern England, covering 6,707 square kilometres (2,950 square miles), Devon has a population of 1,143,000 people in the 2011 Census: barely enough to fill one big city.

The name Devon derives from the ancient 'Dumnonia', which was home to the independent kingdom of Brythonic Celtic-speaking people who inhabited this area of the south-western peninsula of Britain continuously from the Roman era until its partial absorption into the English-speaking Kingdom of Wessex in the eighth or ninth century, with some emigration to the sister Kingdom of Domnonee in Brittany taking place.

The history of Devon can be traced back to the Stone Age, with flint tools found in gravels near Axminster, and other sites, with signs of habitation, in the coastal caves of Torquay, Brixham and Plymouth. Iron Age invaders, crossing the sea from Brittany, established themselves first near the estuaries of the south-east coast and then penetrated to the borders of Dartmoor, the largest open space in southern England.

No traces of the Roman conquest have been found in Devon. The *Dumnonii*, unlike the Durotriges of Dorset, seem to have submitted peacefully as tributary allies. Devon was still less populous than the lands to the eastward, and less wealthy. Its minerals were not exploited during Roman times and the damper inland climate made Dartmoor uninhabitable, while encouraging forest growth over otherwise usable soils. Some sea-trade seems to have carried on from Exeter and Topsham, though land-owners and merchants were not prosperous enough to fully enjoy Roman life, with only two villas known in the county, both near the border with Dorset.

Exeter, now the county town and cathedral city of Devon, was established when traders set up a shanty town of timber buildings within a few years of the Roman Conquest. More than a thousand Roman coins have been found in the city, indicating its importance as a trading centre. The dates of these coins suggest that the city was at its most prosperous in the first half of the fourth century. However, virtually no coins dated after AD 380 have been found, suggesting a rapid decline.

Some 250 years elapsed between the end of Roman rule and the arrival of the English in Devon. There were too few Britons remaining in Dumnonia to offer serious resistance to the English advance, and there was plenty of land which new settlers could take without the need to fight for it. Devon and Somerset fell quickly into Saxon hands, with the 'Red Earth' lands being an obvious attraction. In 682, the Anglo-Saxon Chronicle tells us, King Centwine 'drove the Britons as far as the sea', implying the overrunning of the county as far as the Atlantic coast. The new settlers were great axe-men and they began clearing the valleys, carving farms out of forest and wastelands. They founded large villages, small hamlets and isolated farms where land was plentiful.

Though Devon saw little of the Viking invasion, it was repeatedly raided and sometimes invaded with force during the two long Danish Wars. Tavistock Abbey was destroyed in 997, and in 1001 the Danes ravaged the lower Teign before being beaten off in Exeter.

In the four centuries between the arrival of the English and the Norman Conquest, nearly all of Devon's villages and hamlets were founded. The foundations of Devon, as distinct from Celtic Dumnonia, were solidly laid for the future by generations of pioneering efforts.

Tavistock Church and abbey ruins.

## 1.4 Cornwall

The area now known as Cornwall was first inhabited in the Palaeolithic and Mesolithic periods. It continued to be occupied by Neolithic and then Bronze Age people, and later, in the Iron Age, by Brythons with distinctive cultural relations with neighbouring Wales and Brittany. There is little evidence that Roman rule was effective west of Exeter, and few Roman remains have been found.

Cornwall was occupied by a division of the Dumnonii tribe known as the Cornovii, separated from the Brythons of Wales after the Battle of Deorham, who often came into conflict with the expanding English kingdom of Wessex before King Athelstan, in AD 936, set the boundary between the English and the Cornish at the Tamar.

The name Cornwall is likely to have derived from a combination of two different terms from separate languages. The Roman term for the Celtic tribe which inhabited what is now Cornwall at the time of Roman rule in Britain, Cornovii, came from a Brythonic tribal name from which derives the modern Cornish *Kernow*, known as *Corneu* to the Brythons. This could come from either of two sources: the common Celtic root *cern*, or the Latin *cornu*, both of which mean 'horn' or 'peninsula', suggestive of the shape of Cornwall's landmass.

Cornwall has only one land border, with the county of Devon to its east, and forms the tip of the south-west peninsula of Great Britain, being exposed to the full force of the prevailing winds from the Atlantic Ocean. Its border with Devon is marked for most of its length by the River Tamar and hence the county is almost completely surrounded by water. The coasts of Cornwall have varied characteristics, with the north coast being much more exposed and wilder in nature than the south coast, which is more sheltered with broad estuaries and picturesque fishing villages. The coastline provided plentiful opportunities in the seafaring trades, and the Cornish were true masters of smuggling for hundreds of years.

The only city in the county is Truro, which is the administrative centre for a population of 535,300 individuals (according to the 2011 Census), in an area of 3,563 square kilometres (1,376 square miles). The interior of the county consists of a roughly east–west spine of infertile and exposed upland, with a series of granite intrusions, such as Bodmin Moor.

*Chapter 2*

# TOWN AND COUNTRY

The counties of the West Country are a mix of highly populated cities, market towns, small villages, hamlets and isolated farms, each with their own individual character. Many large country houses are also located within the region, along with architectural structures of great historical importance. It would be impossible to highlight every noteworthy place within the region. So, taking each county individually, some of the main towns and cities are introduced, with an insight into some of the lesser known parishes and their inhabitants. Further recommended reading on this topic can be found in the bibliography for this chapter.

## 2.1  The City of Bristol, its suburbs and hamlets

At the head of the Avon Gorge, Bristol was founded in Saxon times and soon became a major port and market centre. By the eleventh century it had its own mint and was trading with ports throughout western Europe, Wales and Ireland. In the Middle Ages it expanded further as a trading centre and at one time was second only to London as a seaport, exporting raw wool and woollen cloth and importing wines from Spain and France. It was around this time that the River Frome was diverted into a wide artificial channel to form St Augustine's Reach – a remarkable achievement for its day and crucial to the city's development. Later in the nineteenth century Napoleonic prisoners of war, using only picks and shovels, created a semi-artificial waterway, the Floating Harbour, by diverting the course of the River Avon to the south.

For many people Bristol's most famous structure is the Clifton Suspension Bridge that spans the Avon Gorge to the west of the city centre. Opened in 1864, five years after the death of its designer, Isambard Kingdom Brunel, the bridge is suspended 60 metres (200ft) above the river and is a major route into the city.

Clifton suspension bridge.

To the north of Clifton is the suburb of Westbury on Trym, the home of Westbury College Gatehouse, a fifteenth-century gatehouse to the now demolished College of Priests founded in the thirteenth century. Further north is Blaise Hamlet, a tiny hamlet of nine detached and individual stone cottages designed by John Nash in 1809.

## 2.2 Somerset cities

Bath was granted city status by royal charter by Queen Elizabeth I in 1590, having been first established as a spa with the Latin name *Aquae Sulis* ('the waters of Sulis') by the Romans sometime in the first century AD, about twenty years after they arrived in Britain (AD 43). The Romans built baths and a temple on the surrounding hills of Bath, in the valley of the River Avon around hot springs. By the third century the spa had become so renowned that high-ranking soldiers and officials were travelling to Bath from all over the Roman Empire. Within a few years of the Roman legions leaving the city, the drainage systems failed and the area returned to marshland. Ironically, the ancient baths remained hidden for the entire period of Bath's eighteenth-century renaissance and were only discovered in the late nineteenth century.

The building of the present great church began in 1499, after its Norman predecessor had been destroyed by fire, but work was halted at the time of the Dissolution and the church remained without a roof for

The Roman baths.

seventy-five years. Indeed, it was not finally completed until 1901. However, Bath Abbey is now considered to be the ultimate example of Perpendicular church architecture. Inside there is a memorial to Richard 'Beau' Nash, one of the people responsible for turning Bath into a popular Georgian spa town. In the early eighteenth century, before the arrival of Nash, farm animals roamed Bath's streets within the confines of the old Roman town.

A cathedral city, Wells is situated on the southern edge of the Mendip Hills and has enjoyed city status since 1205. It is the second smallest English city in terms of area and population after the City of London, although, unlike the latter, Wells is not part of a larger metropolitan conurbation, and is consequently described in some sources as England's smallest city. The present cathedral was begun about 1175 by Bishop Reginald de Bohun. Built entirely in the new Gothic style, and culminating in the magnificent West Front, the church was largely complete at the time of its dedication to St Andrew in 1239. The castle green is surrounded by a high wall breached at only three castellated entrance points. One of these, the gateway to the Market Place, is known as 'Penniless Porch'; here the bishop allowed the poor of the city to beg for money from those entering the cathedral close.

In 1348 Bishop Ralph of Shrewsbury founded a college for the Vicars Choral, the singing men of the choir, and provided each of the forty-two

Wells Cathedral.

vicars with his own small house. Vicars' Close, as the street came to be known, is the only completely medieval street in England.

## 2.3 Somerset towns and villages

An ancient inland port and industrial town, Bridgwater was established in medieval times at the lowest bridging point of the River Parrett. The settlement that grew up around the castle after the Norman Conquest was little more than a village until the international trade in wool, wheat and other agricultural products began in the Middle Ages. The town grew until at one point it was the most important town on the coast between Bristol and Barnstaple, and in the medieval era, when the town was enormously prosperous, Bridgwater was the fifth busiest port in the country.

Before the canal dock was constructed in the nineteenth century, ships arriving in Bridgwater tied up on both sides of the river below the town's medieval bridge. The decline of the textile industry saw the town undergoing something of a renaissance as new trades were established in the early nineteenth century. When the canal terminus was built, complete with docks and warehouses, the river mud caused the decline of the town's port, but it also had many benefits; when baked in oblong blocks, for example, the mud proved to be an excellent scourer, and these 'Bath Bricks' were used for nearly a century to clean stone and granite steps.

Although a settlement was founded here in the eighth century, the town of Taunton, 12 miles from Bridgwater, has only been the sole centre of administration in Somerset since 1935, with both Ilchester and Somerton previously being the county towns. Like many other West Country towns and villages, Taunton was a thriving wool (and later silk) cloth-making centre during the Middle Ages. Medieval clothiers put all their profits into buildings, and their wealth ensured the construction of two huge churches, St James's and St Mary's.

Some 2 miles south-west of the town lies the village of Norton Fitzwarren, the Roman settlement of Theodunum. The village's antiquity and former importance gave rise to an old rhyme used in several West Country town rivalries: 'When Taunton was a furzy down, Norton was a market town.' Today, although the village has all but been consumed by its much larger neighbour, it has still managed to retain its individuality.

The land around the village of Norton Fitzwarren has always been damp and fertile, and for hundreds of years cider apples have been grown there. The Reverend Thomas Cornish, a local clergyman, first brought cider to the attention of the rest of the nation, when he produced a drink so appetizing that it found great favour with Queen Victoria. Subsequently the cider apples have been transported around the world.

## 2.4 Devon cities

The population of Devon is concentrated in the south of the county, where its two main cities, Exeter and Plymouth, are located. The rural villages of Devon generally have just one parish church, whereas Exeter is divided into twenty-five ecclesiastical parishes. Exeter is described in Barclay's *Complete and Universal English Dictionary* (1842):

> The environs of the city are hilly, and afford a variety of delightful prospects. Its port is properly at Topsham, 5 miles below, but vessels of 150 tons come up to the quay here. Here is a noble cathedral ... court-houses, public institutions for charity and education, &c. It is the seat of an extensive foreign and domestic commerce, and particularly it had a share in the fisheries of Newfoundland and Greenland. Here are flourishing manufactories of serges and other woollen goods. It is seated on the river Exe, over which it has a long stone bridge. It is 173 miles from London ... Population 31,312.

With many fine old buildings, excellent museums and a magnificent cathedral, Exeter can boast a history that goes back over two thousand years, to before the time of the Roman invasion. The city's main street was already in place at this time as it formed part of the ancient trackway which crossed the West Country. After the Romans withdrew from the country, the city became a major ecclesiastical centre and in AD 670 King Cenwealh founded an abbey on the site where the cathedral now stands. The Vikings ransacked and occupied Exeter twice before being driven out by King Alfred. Following the Battle of Hastings William the Conqueror took control of Exeter after a siege lasting eighteen days.

The city is host to many other historical buildings, including the remarkable Guildhall, which was used as a town hall since it was built in 1330, and Tucker's Hall, built in 1471 for the Company of Weavers, Fullers and Shearmen.

The largest centre of population in the south-western peninsula, Plymouth developed at the end of the twelfth century when its potential as a military and commercial port was recognized. However, it was not until the sixteenth century that it became the main base for the English Navy; Sir Francis Drake (a native of Tavistock, see section 2.5, below) famously finished his game of bowls here before leading the fleet from Plymouth against the Spanish Armada.

Portrait of Sir Francis Drake, 1786.

One of the 'three towns', in 1914 Plymouth merged with Devonport, the home of the Royal Naval Dockyard, and Stonehouse, to form what would become the City of Plymouth in 1928. Plymouth was heavily bombed during the Second World War, so much so that the city centre was rebuilt to the designs of Sir Patrick Abercrombie in the 1950s. Still an important commercial centre today, Plymouth boasts one of the country's great stately homes, Saltram House, which overlooks the River Plym. Now in the hands of the National Trust, the house was used as the location for Norland House in the film of Jane Austen's novel *Sense and Sensibility*.

## 2.5 Devon towns and villages

Tavistock is one of Devon's four stannary towns (from the Latin *stannum*: tin). These towns (the others being Ashburton, Chagford and Plympton) were the only places licensed to weigh and stamp the metal extracted from the moor and to collect 'coinage', the tax collected on each ingot of tin, which was passed to the Duchy of Cornwall. A Benedictine abbey was founded in Tavistock in around 974, beside the River Tavy, close to the Saxon stockade, or *stoc*, now incorporated in the town's name. Although little of the abbey remains today, one of its legacies is the annual three-day fair, granted in its charter in 1105. This

Wheal Betsy, part of the Prince Arthur Consols mine.

has evolved into the Goose Fair, a marvellous traditional street fair held in October. Tavistock was also permitted to hold a weekly market; 900 years later this still takes place every Friday.

Some 3 miles north-east of Tavistock the twin villages of Mary Tavy and Peter Tavy lie on opposite banks of the River Tavy, taking their names from the saints of their parish churches. Mary Tavy stands in the heart of the former mining area of Dartmoor, with a survivor from those days lying just north of the village. Wheal Betsy, a restored pumping engine house, was once part of the Prince Arthur Consols mine which produced zinc, silver and lead.

In the churchyard at Mary Tavy is the grave of William Crossing, the historian of the moor, whose guide, first published in the 1900s, is still in print. In 1909 William moved to Peter Tavy, describing it as 'a quiet little place, with a church embosomed by trees, a chapel, a school and a small inn'.

## 2.6 Cornish cities
Situated at the head of a branch of the River Fal, Truro expanded from its ancient roots in medieval times on the prosperity originating from local mineral extraction. It was one of the first towns to be granted the right of Stannary. There are several medieval alleyways which act as a reminder of the times when Truro was a busy port, before the silting up of the river caused Falmouth to take over as the main Cornish port.

The arrival of the railway in 1859 confirmed Truro's status as the regional capital and in 1877 it became a city when Cornwall was granted its own bishop after the division of the diocese of Exeter.

## 2.7 Cornish towns and villages
On the eastern edge of Bodmin Moor, close to the county border with Devon, Launceston (pronounced locally as 'Lan-son') is one of the most rewarding of the county's inland towns. It was a particular favourite of Sir John Betjeman. The capital of Cornwall until 1838, Launceston guarded the main overland route into the county. Robert of Mortain, William I's half-brother, built Launceston Castle shortly after the Norman Conquest, overlooking the River Kensey. Visited by the Black Prince and seized by Cornish rebels in 1549, the castle changed hands twice in the Civil War before becoming an assize court and prison. Launceston was also home to a powerful Augustinian priory, founded beside the river in 1136; although these buildings have now gone, its chapel of ease, St Thomas's Church, remains. The parish church of St Mary Magdalene sits within the town centre with a unique

sixteenth-century exterior of granite carvings of roses, ferns and other motifs.

In the Middle Ages the only dwelling in Bude was Efford Manor, the seat of the Arundells of Trerice, which had a chapel dedicated to St Leonard. However, the town expanded rapidly after the opening of the canal to Launceston in 1820, with the addition of the parish church of St Michael and All Angels (built in 1835 and enlarged in 1876), Ebbingford Manor and the town's oldest house, Quay Cottage, in the centre of town. Bude Castle was built in around 1830, designed by the Victorian inventor Sir Goldsworthy Gurney.

In the latter part of Queen Victoria's reign the middle classes were discovering the attractions of sea bathing, and the Romantic Movement encouraged an appreciation of wild scenery and the Arthurian legends. To serve their aspirations, a railway line was extended to Bude in 1898, making the town a popular holiday destination and busy north Cornwall port.

Just inland from Bude, in an area characterized by small fields, old farmsteads and isolated churches, lies Stratton. A local saying at Stratton is 'Stratton was a market town when Bude was just a furzy down', meaning Stratton was long established when Bude was just gorse-covered downland, and this is certainly supported by the historical buildings of the town, with the twelfth-century Norman church dedicated to St Andrew holding a central and elevated position within

Stratton village.

Stratton Village.

Stratton. The Grade I listed church also contains a brass to Sir John Arundell of Trerice (1561).

As well as the main church, there were various other chapels around the village; this indicates a large population because one church would not suffice. This is also supported by the existence of the large tithe barn – it needed to be large enough to hold the tithes that all villagers paid to the church in the form of one-tenth of their earnings/produce. The area around Cot Hill was an important sanctuary for pilgrims following the pilgrimage route to Hartland during medieval times. However, many of the chapels are now derelict or have been converted to dwellings, suggesting that a decline in population required only the church of St Andrew and one remaining chapel.

One mile north of Bude is the hamlet of Poughill, which is mentioned in the Domesday Book as 'Pochelle'. Notable old houses in Poughill include the medieval Burshill Manor, an open hall house, and the sixteenth-century Church House. The village's water-mill is located on the footpath towards the hamlet of Bush. Lying at the foot of Trevalgus Hill in thick woodland, it is believed to have been a manorial mill for Trevalgus Manor. The mill was powered by the stream called the Stratt which runs south towards Stratton. Part of the mill building was constructed of timbers from ships wrecked along the coastline.

*Chapter 3*

# POPULATION: GROWTH AND DISTRIBUTION CHANGES SINCE 1801

In England various population counts have taken place since the Domesday survey of 1086. However, they only took place on a local basis. The first national census taken in England, Scotland and Wales was in 1801, in response to the threat of invasion by Napoleon. It was designed mainly to ascertain how many men were available for conscription to the army. The results of the 1801 Census for England and Wales showed a population of 8,893,000; by 1811 this figure had risen to 10,164,000, triggering panic that the population explosion would overwhelm the country! In reality, the increase was in no small part due to more efficient enumeration. The population figures were recalculated by order of the government, by adding in the ratio of one to thirty prior to 1811 and one to fifty to the returns made from the districts in the 1811 and 1821 Censuses, to include people in the army and navy.

Censuses have been taken every decade since then, with the exception of 1941, when the government was preoccupied with defending the country in the Second World War. Until 1841 they remained as simple head counts, although in some cases enumerators chose to write down the names and even occupations of the inhabitants. During the eighteenth and nineteenth centuries the demographics of the counties of the West Country show dramatic growth and changes in the distribution of the population within the region.

## 3.1 The City of Bristol

By the twelfth century Bristol was already an important port, handling much of England's trade with Ireland, including slaves. After London, Bristol was one of England's three largest medieval towns in the fourteenth century, along with York and Norwich, and it has been suggested that between a third and half of the population of Bristol died during the Black Death of 1348–49. The plague resulted in a prolonged pause in the growth of its population, with numbers remaining between 10,000 and 12,000 through most of the fifteenth and sixteenth centuries.

Renewed growth came with the seventeenth-century rise of England's American colonies and the rapid eighteenth-century expansion of England's part in the Atlantic trade in Africans taken for slavery in the Americas. During the height of the slave trade, from 1700 to 1807, more than 2,000 slaving ships were fitted out at Bristol, carrying a (conservatively) estimated half a million people from Africa to the Americas and slavery.

Competition from Liverpool from around 1760, the disruption of maritime commerce caused by wars with France (1793) and the abolition of the slave trade (1807) all contributed to the city's failure to keep pace with the newer manufacturing centres of the north of England and the West Midlands, and Bristol's population decreased slightly as its workforce had to journey to pastures new to find employment.

### 3.1.1 Population changes in the nineteenth century

Bristol's population (66,000 in 1801) quintupled during the nineteenth century, supported by new industries and growing commerce. This was particularly associated with the noted Victorian engineer Isambard Kingdom Brunel, who designed and supervised the building of the Great Western Railway between Bristol and London Paddington, two pioneering Bristol-built ocean-going steamships, the SS *Great Britain* and SS *Great Western*, and the Clifton Suspension Bridge. The copper, brass and glass industries went into decline but on the other hand shipbuilding boomed, as did chocolate and soap manufacturing. Connected by waterway, turnpike road and rail, Bristol's cotton and tobacco trades also prospered in the later nineteenth century and in 1891 Bristol had a population of nearly 300,000 residents.

### 3.1.2 Population changes in the twentieth century

By 1901 some 325,000 people were living in Bristol and the city grew steadily as the twentieth century progressed. The city's docklands were enhanced in the early 1900s with the opening of Royal Edward Dock. Another new dock – Royal Portbury Dock – was opened in the 1970s.

With the advent of air travel, aircraft manufacturers set up base at new factories in the city during the first half of the twentieth century.

Bristol suffered heavily from Luftwaffe air raids in the Second World War, claiming the lives of some 1,300 people living and working in the city, with nearly 100,000 buildings being damaged, at least 3,000 of them beyond repair.

The city's education system received a major boost in 1909 with the formation of the University of Bristol, though it really took off in 1925 when its main building was opened. A polytechnic was opened in 1969 to give the city a second higher education institute, which would become the University of the West of England in 1992.

In contrast to the declining population of the remote countryside, there was a vast increase in the size of Bristol, partly due to the expansion of the city boundaries, reaching a peak in 1955 of 445,000 residents. More and more houses were necessary to accommodate the growing city, which stretched out into south Gloucestershire and north Somerset. As the city invaded the countryside, the need for open spaces was soon recognized and now the people of Bristol enjoy some 3,000 acres of fine open downs and parks.

In 2008 the Office for National Statistics (ONS) estimated the Bristol unitary authority's population at 416,900, making it the 47th largest county in England. Using 2001 Census data, the ONS estimated the population of the city to be 441,556, and that of the contiguous urban area to be 551,066. This makes Bristol England's sixth most populous city and ninth most populous urban area. At 3,599 inhabitants per square kilometre (9,321 per square mile), it has the seventh highest population density of any English district. The table below highlights the ethnic groups represented in the City of Bristol in 2009, compared with the national averages for England:

|  | City of Bristol | England |
|---|---|---|
| White | 86.5% | 87.5% |
| Asian or Asian British | 5.2% | 6.0% |
| Black or Black British | 3.4% | 2.9% |
| Mixed race | 2.4% | 1.9% |
| Chinese | 1.5% | 0.8% |
| Other | 1.1% | 0.8% |

## 3.2 Somerset

The first 'head count' census in 1801 shows 273,750 people resident in the county of Somerset, with 10 per cent of these individuals inhabiting the city of Bath. In the preceding century the population had increased by 44 per cent, above the national average and probably due to the considerable produce and manufacturing possibilities, as well as the coastal business carried on from some of the county's ports.

### 3.2.1 Population changes in the nineteenth century

Coal-mining was an important industry in north Somerset in the eighteenth and nineteenth centuries and by 1800 it was especially prominent in Radstock, 9 miles south-west of the city of Bath, with the town's population doubling between 1801 and 1831. Tonnage increased throughout the century with seventy-nine separate collieries producing some 1.25 million tons per annum. Agriculture was also important, with hemp, flax, teasels and woad cultivated in considerable quantities, not to mention the dairies producing some of the finest cheese in the world. Bartholomew's *Gazetteer of the British Isles* (1887) states that 'the principal manufactures are woollen and worsted goods, gloves, lace, linen, crape, silk, paper, glass, and bath-bricks. There are salmon, herring, and other fisheries in the Bristol Channel ...' and naturally the population moved to where their trades could be plied.

Comparing the cities, towns and villages discussed in Sections 2.5 and 2.6, the increase in the populations of the towns of Taunton and Bridgwater far exceeded the swell in the cities between 1801 and 1831, increasing in size by 115 and 92 per cent respectively, although this rise slowed in the mid-nineteenth century, in line with the rest of the county of Somerset.

This century saw improvements to Somerset's roads, with the introduction of turnpikes, and the building of canals and railways. This augmented the employment possibilities within the villages and towns and strengthened the communities within the county, as the inhabitants did not need to migrate to other parishes for work.

In 1891 Somerset's population stood at 484,326, representing just less than 2 per cent of the total population of England, compared to 3 per cent in 1801.

### 3.2.2 Population changes in the twentieth century

Somerset suffered from geological difficulties and, strangely, a shortage of manpower in the mining industry at the turn of the century and the

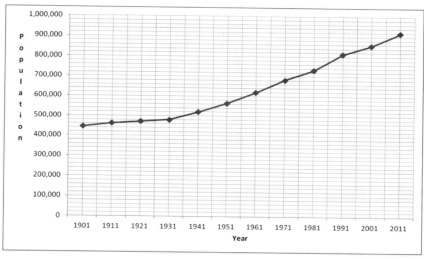

Graph to show the changing population in Somerset, 1901 to 2011.

number of pits declined from thirty to just fourteen by the mid-1930s. The county also lost nearly 5,000 men from the Somerset Light Infantry in the First World War, with war memorials erected in most of the county's towns and villages; only nine, described as the 'Thankful Villages', had none of their residents killed.

During the twentieth century the population grew steadily in Somerset. The growth has been higher than the national average in the last thirty years, with a 6 per cent increase in the Somerset County Council area since 1991, and a 17 per cent increase since 1981. Somerset has a high indigenous British population, with almost 99 per cent registering as white British and 92 per cent of these as born in the United Kingdom. Chinese is the largest ethnic group, while the black minority ethnic proportion of the total population is almost 3 per cent.

With a population of 917,100 recorded in the 2011 Census, more than 25 per cent of the county's population is now concentrated in Taunton, Bridgwater and Yeovil. The rest of the county is rural and sparsely populated.

### 3.3 Devon
When the first census was taken in 1801, Devon had some 354,400 people out of a total for England of about 8.6 million. This was above the national average for a time before the Industrial Revolution had made its mark outside a few limited areas, and when density still mainly depended on agriculture.

| COUNTIES OF | POPULATION. | | |
|---|---|---|---|
| | 1.<br>1700 | 2.<br>1750 | 3.<br>1801 |
| BEDFORD - - - - - - - - | 48,500 | 53,900 | 65,500 |
| BERKS - - - - - - - - | 74,700 | 92,700 | 112,800 |
| BUCKINGHAM - - - - - | 80,500 | 90,700 | 111,000 |
| CAMBRIDGE - - - - - - | 76,000 | 72,000 | 92,300 |
| CHESTER - - - - - - | 107,000 | 131,600 | 198,100 |
| CORNWALL - - - - - - | 105,800 | 135,000 | 194,500 |
| CUMBERLAND - - - - - - | 62,300 | 86,900 | 121,100 |
| DERBY - - - - - - - | 93,800 | 109,500 | 166,500 |
| DEVON - - - - - - - | 248,200 | 272,200 | 354,400 |
| DORSET - - - - - - - | 90,000 | 96,400 | 119,100 |
| DURHAM - - - - - - - | 95,500 | 135,000 | 165,700 |
| ESSEX - - - - - - - - | 159,200 | 167,800 | 234,000 |
| GLOUCESTER - - - - - | 155,200 | 207,800 | 259,100 |
| HEREFORD - - - - - - | 60,900 | 74,100 | 92,100 |
| HERTFORD - - - - - - | 70,500 | 86,500 | 100,800 |
| HUNTINGDON - - - - - | 34,700 | 32,500 | 38,800 |
| KENT - - - - - - - | 153,800 | 190,000 | 317,800 |
| LANCASTER - - - - - | 166,200 | 297,400 | 695,100 |
| LEICESTER - - - - - | 80,000 | 95,000 | 134,400 |
| LINCOLN - - - - - - | 180,000 | 160,200 | 215,500 |
| MIDDLESEX - - - - - | 624,200 | 641,500 | 845,400 |
| MONMOUTH - - - - - | 39,700 | 40,600 | 47,100 |
| NORFOLK - - - - - - | 210,200 | 215,100 | 282,400 |
| NORTHAMPTON - - - - | 119,500 | 123,300 | 136,100 |
| NORTHUMBERLAND - - - | 118,000 | 141,700 | 162,300 |
| NOTTINGHAM - - - - | 65,200 | 77,600 | 145,000 |
| OXFORD - - - - - - - | 79,000 | 92,400 | 113,200 |
| RUTLAND - - - - - - | 16,600 | 13,800 | 16,900 |
| SALOP, (Shropshire) - - - | 101,600 | 130,300 | 172,200 |
| SOMERSET - - - - - - | 195,900 | 224,500 | 282,800 |
| SOUTHAMPTON, (Hampshire) - | 118,700 | 137,500 | 226,900 |
| STAFFORD - - - - - - | 117,200 | 160,000 | 247,100 |
| SUFFOLK - - - - - - | 152,700 | 156,800 | 217,400 |
| SURREY - - - - - - - | 154,900 | 207,100 | 278,000 |
| SUSSEX - - - - - - - | 91,400 | 107,400 | 164,600 |
| WARWICK - - - - - - | 96,600 | 140,000 | 215,100 |
| WESTMORLAND - - - - | 28,600 | 36,300 | 43,000 |
| WILTS - - - - - - - | 153,900 | 168,400 | 191,200 |
| WORCESTER - - - - - | 88,200 | 108,000 | 143,900 |
| YORK, East Riding - - - - | 96,200 | 85,500 | 144,000 |
| D° North Riding - - - | 98,600 | 117,200 | 160,500 |
| D° West Riding - - - | 236,700 | 361,500 | 582,700 |
| ENGLAND - - - - - - | 5,146,400 | 6,073,700 | 8,606,400 |
| WALES - - - - - - - | 366,500 | 449,300 | 559,000 |
| TOTAL - - - - - § | 5,512,900 | 6,523,000 | 9,165,400 |

Census of Great Britain, 1801. Abstract of the answers and returns made pursuant to an Act, passed in the forty-first year of His Majesty King George III.

Opposite is the enumeration abstract for 1801 showing the population for each of the English counties in 1700, 1750 and 1801.

### 3.3.1 *Population changes in the nineteenth century*

In 1801 there were 57,955 inhabited houses recorded in Devon, increasing to 62,318 in 1811 and 71,486 in 1821. The number of families then resident in the county was 90,714, comprising 208,229 males and 230,811 females. There are a number of publications which provide useful guides to the pre-1841 censuses and lists for each county, such as Chapman's *Pre-1841 Censuses & Population Listings in the British Isles* and Gibson and Medlycott's *Local Census Listings 1522–1930*.

With the encouragement of the Devon County Archivist, John Draisey, a GENUKI/Devon transcription project has been set up with the aim of identifying all the extant pre-1841 Devon censuses and population listings, making transcripts or indexes available online in GENUKI/Devon or supplying references to known indexes held by the Devon Family History Society, archives or libraries.

The increase in population from 1801 to 1831 was neither consistent throughout the county nor throughout the decades, as the table below shows, using the cities, towns and villages discussed in Sections 2.1 and 2.2.

| Parish, township, etc | Population | | | | 1801–1831 |
|---|---|---|---|---|---|
| | 1801 | 1811 | 1821 | 1831 | % increase |
| Exeter | 17,398 | 18,896 | 22,989 | 28,201 | 62% |
| Mary Tavy | 376 | 631 | 933 | 1,123 | 199% |
| Peter Tavy | 221 | 294 | 358 | 500 | 126% |
| Plymouth | 43,194 | 56,060 | 61,212 | 75,534 | 75% |
| Tavistock | 3,420 | 4,723 | 5,483 | 5,602 | 64% |

Note: All percentage increases are rounded to the nearest integer value.

Although more populous from the outset, the percentage increase in the number of inhabitants in the cities and larger towns of Devon is surpassed by that in the small farming villages.

White's *Devonshire Directory* (1850) states:

TAVY ST MARY, or Mary Tavy, a scattered village in the Tavy valley, and on the western side of Dartmoor, 4 miles N.E. by N. of Tavistock, is mostly inhabited by miners. Its parish contains 1552 souls, and 4180 acres of land, including about 2100A. of open moorland; the village of Horndon; the high moorland district of Black Down, and other parts of Dartmoor, where there are five valuable copper, tin, and lead mines, called Wheal, and North, South, and East Wheal Friendship ...

TAVY ST PETER, a scattered village in the Tavy valley, on the western borders of Dartmoor, 4 miles N.N.E. of Tavistock, has in its parish 587 souls, and about 6000 acres of land, of which 91 souls, and about 2450 acres, are in *Willsworthy* hamlet, a high moorland district in Lifton Hundred, 6 miles N.N.E. of Tavistock. The parish also includes *Godsworthy*, and many scattered farm houses.

The population of the county of Devon is stated in Barclay's *Complete and Universal English Dictionary* (1842) as 533,460 in 1842, rising to 567,000 in the 1851 Census, according to Sellman's *Illustrations of Devon History*: an increase of 60 per cent in fifty years, while the whole country's population had risen by nearly 100 per cent over the same period. The great coal-based industrial towns that had grown elsewhere had no counterpart in Devon. Instead, their competition helped to extinguish what remained of industry in the county. However, agriculture was still flourishing and, apart from the port towns, including Exeter, it still governed the distribution of population in Devon.

Labourers' wages were abominably low in Devon, even by the standards of the time, and farmers could afford to employ as many as they could find a use for. The prosperity of farming also supported local markets, tradesmen and craftsmen in the smaller inland towns.

The next fifty years saw Devon's population rise by less than 17 per cent compared to a national increase of over 77 per cent, and this increase was in the urban areas. There was a depression in farming in the 1870s, largely brought about by competition from cheap imported grain, and the small villages and towns lost between a third and a quarter of their inhabitants. The parishes of Mary Tavy and Peter Tavy decreased to 895 and 309 inhabitants respectively in 1881: less than their population sixty years previously, in the census of 1821.

Much of the land that had previously been cultivated was turned over to grazing for cattle; the lower labour demands meant farmers needed

The Barton, Luffincott, 1908.

fewer workers, and cut back their spending in the local market towns. The areas hit the hardest were the north and north-west of the Devon, where the soil was less fertile, and the rural villages really suffered in the latter part of the nineteenth century.

The impact of the depression is clearly evident within Devon village communities and can be witnessed on an individual farm basis using the nineteenth-century censuses. For example, in 1851 the Barton at Luffincott, 6 miles south of Holsworthy, was occupied by Abraham Trible, his wife, two sons and an aunt. Abraham had four farm labourers, along with his two sons, farming the 200 acres of land. By 1881 the Barton was occupied by the Congdon family, with no sons of an age to assist with farm duties and just two farm servants.

However, by comparison, the holiday resorts and retirement areas of the south coast grew out of all proportion. Torquay more than doubled, Paignton trebled and, as the port and dockyard developed, the 'three towns' of Plymouth, Devonport and Stonehouse nearly doubled in size.

### 3.3.2 Population changes in the twentieth century

For the first part of the twentieth century the trends which had developed in the latter part of the nineteenth century continued. Except during the First World War, the depression in farming was unrelenting, with the revival in 1939 coinciding with mechanization and an increase in labour costs. As a consequence, the resurgence in the agricultural industry made little difference to employment levels. Inland villages barely held their own, with many declining yet further, unless they were lucky enough to have another employment source such as a factory, quarry or similar.

The development of motorized vehicles made it simpler for people to live at a distance from their place of work, and the villages close to large towns have sometimes grown as a result. However, this has caused inland centres to suffer yet further. Today, nearly half the total population of the county of Devon live in Plymouth, Exeter and the Torbay towns.

## 3.4 Cornwall

Cornwall had only a little over half the population of Devon in 1801 with its inhabitants numbering 194,500, three times the number of residents of the City of Bristol, including its suburbs. Pigot et al's *British Atlas: Counties of England* (1840) states that 'Cornwall, from its soil, appearance and climate, is one of the least inviting of the English counties ... The saltness of the atmosphere, and the violence of the winds, will scarcely suffer trees, or even hedges, to grow near the shore; so that nearly the whole county presents a naked and almost desolate appearance.'

### 3.4.1 Population changes in the nineteenth century

The number of inhabited houses in Cornwall increased by 33 per cent from 1801 to 1821, in comparison to a 23 per cent increase in Devon. However, Cornwall had less than two-thirds of the number of dwellings in Devon in 1821, most likely due to the isolated nature of the region. Until the railway crossed the Tamar at Plymouth in 1859, there were few roads to Cornwall and no track worthy of such a name when you arrived there.

The population of the county was more evenly distributed than its neighbour's as it lacked the presence of large cities and towns, with Truro boasting just 2,925 inhabitants in 1821. The villages and towns of Cornwall show a higher percentage increase in inhabitants over the first thirty years of the nineteenth century when compared with Truro, with the population of the village of Stratton expanding by 68 per cent. However, when comparing Stratton to Mary Tavy in Devon (nearly 200 per cent in the same period) the development within the village appears less remarkable.

Tin and copper mines were dispersed throughout the greater part of Cornwall and it is said that the quantity of tin produced in the county was greater than in any other part of the world in the 1840s. The areas of Cornwall around Gwennap and St Day and on the coast around Porthtowan were among the richest mining areas in the world, and at its height the Cornish tin-mining industry had around 600 steam engines working to pump out the mines (many mines stretched out under the sea and some went down to great depths). However, foreign competition depressed the price of copper, and later tin, to a level that made Cornish ores unprofitable. By the middle and late nineteenth century Cornish mining was in decline, and many Cornish miners emigrated overseas to developing mining districts, where their skills were in great demand: these included South Africa, Australia and North America. Cornish miners became dominant in the 1850s in the iron and copper districts of northern Michigan in the United States, as well as in many other mining areas. In the first six months of 1875 more than 10,000 miners left Cornwall to find work overseas, significantly decreasing the inland population of the county.

Sea-bathing became popular in the mid-eighteenth century and Cornwall was quick to gain recognition as a holiday destination; from the early nineteenth century Bude became a popular watering-place while Penzance drew comparisons with the French Riviera. Certainly the equable climate lured in well-off invalids, especially in winter. With improved transportation to the region in the 1850s and 1860s, seaside trips became available for the first time to ordinary working people and this resulted in a continual expansion of the coastal towns and villages of Cornwall. The fine golden sandy beaches of the north coast attracted visitors and boosted the tourist industry, particularly in Newquay and Bude, and the more sheltered south coast of the county, with its several broad estuaries, offered safe anchorage in Falmouth and Fowey to those holidaying by sea. The picturesque fishing village of Polperro and the port of Looe also caught the attention of middle-class Victorians.

In 1891, the last census of the nineteenth century, Cornwall's inhabitants totalled just 322,589 – 1 per cent of England's population of 27.5 million.

### 3.4.2 *Population changes in the twentieth century*

As the industries of the previous century largely declined, the workers of Cornwall found themselves in distress or obliged to leave the region to find work elsewhere, and the turn of the century saw a decline in the population of this county. It was not until after the Second World War that Cornwall saw its population return to the same level as a hundred years previously.

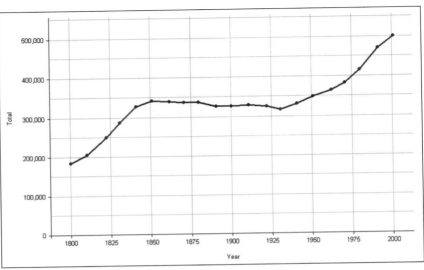

Graph to show the change in population in Cornwall between 1800 and 2000.

Improvements in infrastructure and transportation in the mid-twentieth century saw further expansion in the tourist industry and a slight increase in the employment opportunities for people within the region. The county depends heavily on tourism, which accounts for around a quarter of Cornwall's economy.

Cornwall is 99.0 per cent White British and has seen a relatively high level of population growth in the last thirty years. At 11 per cent in the 1980s and 5 per cent in the 1990s, it has the fifth highest population growth of the English counties. Many people's choice of Cornwall for their retirement has augmented the population but Cornwall is still recognized as one of the poorest counties in the country. Official measures of deprivation and poverty at district and 'sub-ward' level show that there is great variation in poverty and prosperity in Cornwall, with some areas ranking among the poorest in England and others among the top half in prosperity. For example, the ranking of 32,482 sub-wards in England in the index of multiple deprivation (2006) ranged from 819th (part of Penzance East) to 30,899th (part of Saltash Burraton in Caradon), where the lower number represents the greater deprivation.

In the 2011 Census Cornwall's inhabitants numbered 535,300, which ranked its population thirty-ninth out of the forty-eight counties of England.

## 3.5 Digging deeper

The Online Historical Population Reports (OHPR) collection (www.histpop.org) provides online access to the complete British population reports for Britain and Ireland from 1801 to 1937. The collection goes far beyond basic population reports, with a wealth of textual and statistical material providing an in-depth view of the economy, society (through births, deaths and marriages) and medicine during the nineteenth and early twentieth centuries.

These 200,000 pages of census and registration material for the British Isles are supported by numerous ancillary documents from the National Archives, critical essays and transcriptions of important legislation which provide an aid to understanding the context, content and creation of the collection.

More information about where our forebears lived can be gained from maps of the region. Most records are arranged geographically and when a village, town or city is located, maps help to visualise the surrounding area. By examining a series of historical maps of the county in which your ancestor lived, the growth of the area can be seen in relation to the roads, canals, railways, bridges and so forth, as well as, with the progress of the Industrial Revolution, the diminishing of the forest. Held at county record offices and local libraries, these maps can often be supplemented with contemporary photographs held at the same location.

There are several online gazetteers for locating places, including the Ordnance Survey, the Association of British Counties Gazetteer of British Place Names, Archaeology UK Place Name Search, GENUKI and the Vision of Britain websites.

Many seventeenth-century maps are in the House of Lords Record Office and each county record office holds collections relevant to their area. J. Bell's *A New and Comprehensive Gazetteer of England and Wales* (1834) is reproduced in the *Phillimore Atlas and Index* (2003), along with maps showing the borders of parishes and ecclesiastical jurisdictions.

The original Ordnance Survey maps for the British Isles are fascinating and can be examined at local libraries, museums or county record offices. Full sets are held at the British Library. They are also available from Cassini Maps for a fee.

For the county parishes, there are tithe apportionment maps, covering roughly three-quarters of the English and Welsh parishes, made between 1838 and 1854. Regularizing the payment of tithes, they show and number each field and building. This links to the apportionment schedule, which describes the land and its rentable value, along with the names of the owners and occupiers. Copies are held at county record offices and also in classes IR 29 (schedules) and IR 30 (maps) at the National Archives.

There are many websites offering maps from centuries gone by for researchers to purchase. However, so many maps are available online there is little need to spend any money.

Genmaps is a site devoted to online images of English, Welsh and Scottish maps from their beginnings to the early twentieth century. Most of the images on the website are from scans donated by the owners of old maps. Although the maps shown are free of copyright, the images are not and so any commercial use of the images is expressly forbidden. Other sites are also available, such as Old Maps (www.oldmaps.co.uk), which includes Ordnance Survey mapping.

## 3.6 Hidden treasures

Many of the tithe schedule books have been transcribed, which makes research quicker. The Friends of Devon's Archives tithe apportionment transcription project is one of particular note. Cornwall Record Office has a volunteer transcription project with a CDROM tithe package available at a fee, while the Friends of Somerset Archives have transcribed some apportionments and made them available at the Somerset Heritage Centre.

Tithe map for Tetcott, 1839.

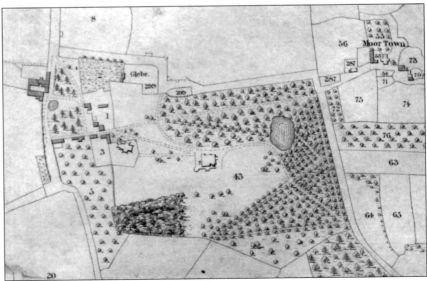

The tithe maps for some areas are available on microfilm or fiche, especially if the originals are in a poor state of repair.

Tetcott tithe map shows the Church Yard Garden (number 3), farm, yard, mowhay and gardens (1), Higher Gardens (2) and orchard (5), owned by Sir William Molesworth, a prosperous land-owner in Devon and Cornwall, and occupied by Francis Chapple.

For modern photographs of the parishes, the online Geograph Britain and Ireland project aims to collect geographically representative photographs and information for every square kilometre of Great Britain and Ireland, and is a 'geography project for the people' where contributors take photographs and upload them to the website.

Many people find that their ancestors do not travel far from their birth roots, particularly in the more rural parishes of the West Country. This can lead to researchers holding many records (transcripts, microfiche and/or copies) for a specific parish and working on a one place study (OPS), developing great knowledge of the historical environment and events large and small that took place within a village. A one place study is a large undertaking and would generally have as its ultimate aim the reconstruction of a definitive family tree for each of the families in their village, as well as analysis of issues like life expectancy and geographical mobility. Known one place studies for each county are listed online with links to research that has been made available by one place studiers. There are many studies being undertaken in the West Country, from Morvah and Madron in the west of Cornwall, via Bucks Mills, Feniton and Westleigh in Devon, to Nailsea and Clevedon in Somerset.

*Chapter 4*

# TRAVEL AND TRANSPORT

In Tudor times the only methods of travel on land were 'shanks's pony' (on foot) or by horse. The 'roads' of the day were simple dirt tracks and thus a journey by horse or horse-drawn carriage was slow and uncomfortable. By law, men were supposed to spend six days per year repairing the local roads. However, very few villagers travelled and therefore they were not particularly interested in performing this task, especially as it seemed to offer them no benefits.

In the sixteenth century you would be lucky if you could travel 45 to 65 kilometres (30 to 40 miles) a day, and it took a week to travel from London to Plymouth. More affluent members of society deliberately travelled slowly as they felt it was undignified to hurry, and so took their time.

Although goods could be transported by pack horse (horses carrying bags or panniers) or on covered wagons, people preferred to transport goods by water. All around England there was a 'coastal trade', with goods being taken by sea from one port to another.

Transport and communications improved in the middle of the seventeenth century, with stagecoaches running regularly between the major towns. However, they were extremely expensive and must have been very uncomfortable without springs on rough roads. There was also the danger of highwaymen.

A private Act of Parliament in 1663 ushered in a change in the administration of the road networks, which would see the repair and maintenance of the highways and, it was hoped, make a profit.

## 4.1 Turnpike roads

The first turnpike trust was established in 1663 to repair and maintain a particularly badly worn 24-kilometre (15-mile) stretch of the Great North Road between Wadesmill and Royston in Hertfordshire and Cambridgeshire. It was not until the 1690s that the number of new

Turnpike Acts rose, with four in the 1690s, to ten in the 1700s (including Bath in 1707), twenty-two in the 1710s and forty-six in the 1720s (including Bristol in 1721). By 1750 most of the major through-routes in England had been turnpiked, although no turnpike roads had yet been authorized in Cornwall, Devon or Dorset. The most active period for the formation of turnpike trusts was between 1751 and 1772, when 389 new Acts were passed; the London road from Exeter was turnpiked in 1753 and from Truro in 1754, with trusts soon set up in most of the towns of the counties of Devon, Cornwall and Somerset to supervise the neighbouring highways.

Making a road into a turnpike was essentially a legal change, rather than a physical one; some acts were never implemented and others were

Turnpike roads, Bristol.

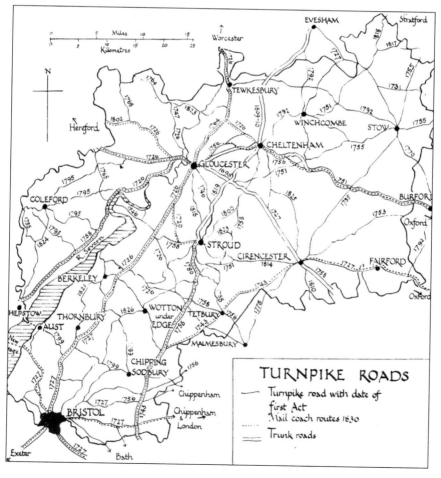

only partly enforced. The amount of effort put into improving a turnpike road might vary considerably from one stretch of the road to another, depending upon the amount of traffic and the tolls generated. At first, the improvement of the roads was often less obvious than the nuisance of paying a toll. Not until after the Battle of Waterloo did John Loudon McAdam's method of surfacing, and the engineering of totally new routes, bring a real revolution and make the full development of coaching possible.

At their peak in the 1830s over a thousand trusts administered around 50,000 kilometres (30,000 miles) of turnpike road in England and Wales, taking tolls at almost 8,000 toll-gates.

### 4.1.1 The City of Bristol

The roads around Bristol, the gateway port of the west, were turnpiked in the first half of the eighteenth century, and the Bath Road, the road from Bristol to London, in 1727. Other acts were passed for the maintenance of the main routes between Bristol and Gloucester, and from each of those cities to the capital, with the formation of the Bridgwater Trust (1730) carrying the Bristol road south across the Somerset Levels.

John McAdam was personally responsible for many local roads in the nineteenth century, as he was the surveyor of the Bristol Turnpike Trust from 1815 to 1824. Together with his son, John Nicholl McAdam, he reformed the administration of the Trust and supervised some 200 road improvements in the Bristol area.

### 4.1.2 Somerset

Somerset sits on the boundary between areas where wealth and topography led to the creation of some of the earliest turnpikes, and the less economically favoured counties of Devon and Cornwall where turnpiking came relatively late. The roads leading into Bath were among the first in England to be turnpiked, in 1707. This was associated with improvements to the roads that carried wealthy travellers between London and this leading leisure resort of post-Restoration England. There was then a gap until the 1750s, when Somerset saw a similar pattern to Devon, Dorset and Cornwall in creating a rush of town-centred turnpike trusts.

Trusts with large mileages were created in Taunton (1752) and Wells (1753) to carry the Bath road across the county. The trusts for Black Dog

(Bath and Warminster) (1752), Shepton Mallet (1753) and Langport (1753), Bruton (1756), Wincanton (1756) and Frome (1757) created a string of turnpikes on a route running to the south of the Post Road. Finally, in the south, the roads around Chard (1759) and Crewkerne (1765) completed the turnpiking of all the main routes after a little over a decade.

Smaller trusts were then created which seemed to be turnpiking every highway in sight with no obvious focus on the main roads. In the south of the county, for example, Martock (1761), Ilminster (1772) and Ilchester (1800) intermingled with the other trust roads to create a thick web of minor turnpikes, and in the west the sparsely populated areas around Exmoor were turnpiked by extensive trusts based in Minehead (1765) and Wiveliscombe (1786).

In the early nineteenth century new roads were built across the Devon border, particularly the Honiton and Ilminster Road (1807), and new routes were turnpiked across Sedgemoor by the High Ham and Ashcott and the Wedmore Trusts in (1826/7) and the Wells and Highbridge Road (1841). Finally Somerset got its road to the seaside in 1840 with the turnpiking of a short section of road to Weston-super-Mare.

As with the other counties of the West Country, the arrival of the railways saw a period of steady decline in the trusts, and in Somerset they were wound up from the late 1870s onwards and the roads transferred to local Highway Boards and subsequently to the County Council in 1888.

### 4.1.3 Devon

The London road from Dorset was turnpiked in sections by urban-centred trusts at Axminster and Honiton (1754 Act), Exeter (1753), Okehampton (1760) and Launceston (1760). The more usual pattern of turnpiking stretches of rural highway, taking tolls from long-distance travellers passing through these parishes, is evident on the roads from Dorchester and Bristol. The naval facilities at Plymouth required supplies from within Devon and a number of turnpike roads were built to serve this. Originally, a Plymouth-centred trust had been proposed, but eventually the responsibility was shared between several trusts: the Plymouth Eastern (1756), the Modbury Trust (1759) covering roads to the east, the Tavistock Trust (1762) dealing with roads from the north, and the Saltash Trust (1762) responsible for the road westwards to the Cremyll Passage over the Tamar. At about the same time roads were turnpiked into the ports of the South Hams: Kingsbridge and

Dartmouth (1759) and Totnes (1762). Later, roads within Plymouth were improved by the Stonehouse Trust (1784).

During the latter part of the eighteenth century roads across Dartmoor were improved by the new Moretonhampstead Trust (1772) and by extensions to the existing Tavistock Roads (1772). A new road was built from Roborough to the prisoner-of-war prison on Dartmoor in 1812, and a north–south route created by the extension of the Newton Bushell Roads in 1826.

Some of the eighteenth-century trusts created new branches of existing roads, to avoid hills and narrow village streets, and several such 'bypasses' on the roads out of Exeter are popular with today's motorist. The old Exeter to Barnstaple route between Crediton and Newbridge was completely replaced by a new road along the Taw Valley, from which new branches were made to Torrington and South Molton.

Coach services reflected these improvements, with properly surfaced roads allowing faster travel in lighter vehicles, the new routes helping to cut journey times significantly. The first mail coaches from London to Exeter in 1785 took just twenty-four hours and by 1824 this had been cut to twenty-two.

Two mail routes were operating through the county by 1787, with one running via Dorchester through Exeter, Okehampton and Launceston (Cornwall) to Falmouth (Cornwall), and the other via Shaftesbury (Dorset) and Exeter through Chudleigh and Ashburton to Devonport. A third route was added in the nineteenth century through Taunton (Somerset), Tiverton, Barnstaple and Bideford to Launceston and Plymouth, which gave a direct connection to Bristol. Regular passenger coach services, apart from the mail coaches, were serving all the chief towns by 1820 and in the 1830s seventy coaches left Exeter every day.

In the early nineteenth century the roads around the seaside resorts of South Devon were turnpiked: Honiton to Sidmouth (1816), Teignmouth and Dawlish (1823), Exmouth (1823) and Dartmouth and Torquay (1825). In North Devon the Barnstaple Trust extended its roads to Ilfracombe in 1828 and a new trust was created at Combe Martin in 1838. However, the north-west of the county remained poorly served by turnpikes; even some of the Bideford turnpike roads were returned to parish control. The traffic on these remote roads was probably insufficient to warrant taking on the financial burden of turnpiking. Although the more affluent residents around Holsworthy had considered turnpiking the main road in 1787, it seems they decided against this and the roads remained toll-free, repaired by a local highways board. The quality of this maintenance was such that in the

1840s the Holsworthy roads were held up as a good example of how Highway Boards could manage roads economically.

When the railways opened, most coach services closed down and roads were suddenly deserted by all but local traffic. However, a few coaches survived in places which the railway never reached and these continued until motor transport took over.

### 4.1.4 Cornwall

The first turnpike act covering Cornish roads was the creation of the Truro Roads in 1754. Sections of the main post road were turnpiked in 1760, the Launceston Trust bringing the road over from Devon, and the Haleworthy Road continuing the route along the northern edge of the county through Camelford and Wadebridge. In quick succession the main town-based trusts were created: Helston, Liskeard, Lostwithiel and St Austell (1761), Creed/St Just and Saltash (1762), Penryn (1763) and Callington (1764). Finally the Bodmin Turnpike Trust was created in 1769, providing a route through the centre of the county, over the moor.

By 1770 there were three turnpiked routes into the county: the road from Okehampton through Launceston, the road over Dartmoor through Tavistock to Callington, and the road from Plymouth across the three ferries on the lower Tamar. These fed three principal roads to Truro: from Launceston through either Wadebridge or Bodmin, and through Liskeard from either Callington or the ferries. Each of these trusts renewed and extended their powers in the subsequent decades. In the early nineteenth century new trusts were created to provide better roads to meet particular mining needs: Trebarwith Sands Road in 1825 to move sand in and slate out, Hayle Causeway in 1825 to 1839 and Penzance and St Just, very late in 1863, to serve the metal ore mines. The north-east of the county had no turnpike trusts but seems to have been served by a very good Highways Board centred on Stratton in Cornwall and Holsworthy in Devon. Traffic levels in this area were probably insufficient to warrant the cost of turnpiking to assist the basic parish road maintenance arrangements.

The Cornwall trusts were affected by the arrival of the railways in the late 1850s and after a period of steady decline were progressively wound up from the late 1870s onwards, with the roads transferred to local Highways Boards and subsequently to the County Council in 1888.

### 4.1.5 Digging deeper

The progress of a private bill through Parliament can be followed in the printed Journals of the House of Commons and House of Lords, and a complete set of acts is available in the House of Lords Record Office, including any renewal acts. Printed acts, naming the trustees and outlining their powers, are usually available in local studies libraries and local record offices. They also have surviving records of turnpike trusts that may include information about employees.

The county maps of the late eighteenth century are an accurate source for tracing the course of turnpike roads and for identifying toll-gates. Travellers' guides such as John Cary's *New Itinerary* (1798) are also a prime source of information. This documentary evidence should be combined with remaining visual 'on the ground' evidence, in particular milestones and toll-keepers' cottages.

### 4.1.6 Hidden treasures

About a quarter of the toll-houses in the West Country still exist, and a fine-looking building built by the Modbury Turnpike Trust in around 1823 can still be seen in Yealmbridge.

Yealmbridge toll-house, South Hams.

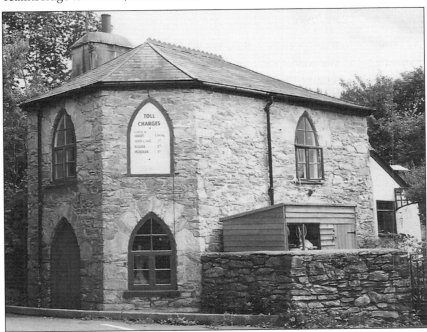

The majority of mile markers in the West Country were milestones, though these differ from county to county, with each trust adopting a different pattern of milestone, presumably because they contracted with local stonemasons who used individual designs. There are more surviving milestones in Cornwall than the total turnpike mileage. In Devon, the Barnstaple Trust, in a final gesture before handing over responsibility of the roads to Highway Boards, commissioned new stones to a common design for the 104 miles of turnpike roads for which it was responsible, and many of these Barum stones survive. Devon is unusual in the number of turnpike terminus stones that have survived, particularly from the Okehampton Trust but also from the Exeter Trust. There are also a few cast-iron mileposts to be found, mainly in the south-west of the county, on roads serving Plymouth.

## 4.2 Railways

Richard Trevithick, a Cornish engineer, built the first steam locomotive for a railway in 1804. Other pioneers of the era included John Blenkinsop and William Hedley, who used steam locomotives to move coal, and George Stephenson who built *Locomotion* for the Stockton & Darlington Railway, which was opened in 1825 for passenger and goods traffic. The famous *Rocket,* which won the Rainhill trials in 1829, was the first steam locomotive designed to pull passenger traffic at speed.

### 4.2.1 The City of Bristol

On many occasions prior to 1832, the citizens of Bristol had considered proposals for the construction of a railway to connect Bristol with London. However, nothing concrete resulted until four influential local businessmen, Thomas Richard Guppy, George Jones, John Harford and William Tothill, in conjunction with Isambard Kingdom Brunel, started a company for constructing a railway. The works that Brunel constructed for the Great Western Railway in the neighbourhood of Bristol were among the most complex. East of the city, bridges had to be built to carry the line over the Floating Harbour, the Feeder Canal and the New Cut. The first trains took just four hours to reach London, compared to between twelve and sixteen by coach.

The Great Western Railway Company erected the first goods depot at Temple Meads in 1840, catering for 209 wagons, and between 1840 and 1860 a network of lines radiated out from Bristol to Gloucester. In 1865 Temple Meads became the hub for the three railway companies (the Great Western, the Midland, and the Bristol & Exeter) then serving Bristol. Temple Meads is described in Morgan's *Guide* in 1849:

A porter is ready to conduct you to the booking office, where you pay your fare and receive a ticket; you then ascend a flight of stairs to the platform. Having taken your place, and made all ready, you are now at ease to observe what is going on … several engines with red hot fires in their bodies, and volumes of condensed steam issuing from them: one of them moves slowly towards you … a whistle is sounded as signal for starting – and you are off.

The presence of a railway line had many lasting effects on the growth of nineteenth-century towns, and for Bristol the rail network served to further improve the trading possibilities of the city and provide better connections for the West Country as a whole.

### 4.2.2 Somerset

The railway came to Somerset in 1840 with the Bath to Bristol line, on the route that is still in use today, completed by the Great Western Railway. The Bristol & Exeter Railway opened its line south of Bristol and the railway arrived in Bridgwater in 1841; this was the terminus of the line for a year while the Somerset Bridge was constructed over the River Parrett. Taunton station opened in July 1842, with the line to Exeter completed in 1844.

The Bristol & Gloucestershire Railway became part of the Midland Railway in 1845, and in 1864 an act was obtained for a branch from Mangotsfield to Bath, which opened in 1869. Two new lines followed from the Bath–Bristol route in 1874: to Clifton Downs (from a junction west of Fishponds) and to Bournemouth in Dorset (from Bath via the Somerset & Dorset Railway).

First authorized in 1857, the West Somerset Railway was opened in 1862 as a broad-gauge line from Norton Fitzwarren, near Taunton, to Watchet. Plans to extend the route to Minehead were launched in 1865, but this was not fulfilled until 1874. Mineral traffic and freight were the line's primary inspiration, along with a desire to open up a part of north Somerset and its coastline that had previously been inaccessible to railway passengers.

The line was converted to standard gauge in 1882 and eventually came under Great Western Railway control. With the emphasis for the line switching to tourism, Watchet, Blue Anchor, Dunster and Minehead had particular appeal for holidaymakers, with firm beaches, rugged cliffs with plentiful caves and wide panoramas.

The route between Watchet and Taunton passed through the Quantock Hills, whose qualities were appreciated by the public in the late nineteenth century with an increasing interest in rambling and exploring the countryside.

### 4.2.3 Devon

Railways came to Devon in a simple form in the early nineteenth century with the Haytor Granite Railway (1820), which was used to transport granite from the quarries at Haytor on Dartmoor. The Dartmoor Railway, from Princetown to Plymouth, started its life three years later in 1823. The Napoleonic wars were over, the prison at Princetown had been closed, and so greater attention was paid to the farmland improvements schemes of Sir Thomas Tyrwhitt, a local land-owner, to sustain the community that had grown up around the prison.

In 1831 civic dignitaries in Bideford and Okehampton had toyed with the idea of constructing a railway line between the two towns. Surveys were carried out and reports published, but it came to nothing. Meanwhile Bristol, which already had a line linking it with London, turned its vision eastward. By 1842 the Bristol & Exeter Railway had reached Taunton, and by 1843 it had been extended a further 12 kilometres (8 miles) to meet the turnpike, so that rail travellers could take a coach to Exeter. The tunnel in the Devon and Somerset border hills was commenced the same year and completed in 1844, when the line through the tunnel reached Exeter.

The South Devon Railway was eventually formed and the Plymouth–Exeter scheme was authorized in 1844. By 1846 the line had reached Teignmouth, and by the end of the year Newton Abbot. By the mid-nineteenth century Devon possessed a through line from Taunton all the way to Plymouth, with a short line from Tiverton Road to Tiverton and another from Newton Abbot to Torquay. In 1851 the Exeter to Crediton line was opened after four years of dispute over what gauge the tracks should be, between the Bristol & Exeter, and London & South Western Railways, which resulted in one broad gauge and one narrow gauge line. The next line of importance in Devon was the Plymouth to Tavistock line, opened in 1859 by the South Devon & Tavistock Railway Company, headed by Lord Morley. Meanwhile the North Devon Company added a line from Barnstaple to Crediton, which eventually reached Torrington in 1872. Many other lengths of line were added in the county in the latter part of the nineteenth century and the early twentieth century, with Devon's main network of railway systems being completed by the beginning of the 1900s. An excellent map of the development of Devon's railways is available in the centre of Helen Harris's *Devon Railways* (2008).

The county as a whole benefited from the rail network. For the first time it was brought into close regular contact with national life, and the railways offered the chance to develop the holiday resorts for tourists, and markets for the produce of horticulture and dairy farming to offset the decline in industry and the slump in cereals. The large centres of Exeter and Plymouth grew rapidly, the latter especially, as railways developed its harbours and suburbs. However, the small inland towns which had previously been the only shopping places for their area suffered greatly when they had to compete with the attraction of the larger centres now accessible by train. Since 1851 much of the population shift in the county can be solely attributed to the railways.

### 4.2.4 Cornwall

In the first half of the nineteenth century Falmouth was an important landing station for shipping, and a number of schemes were developed for a railway connection from the town to London. These did not gain the financial support necessary to make progress, and in 1843 local businessmen W. Tweedy and W.H. Bond approached the Great Western Railway to try to persuade them to fund an extension of the South Devon Railway, then only a *planned* railway, into Cornwall. Direct assistance was refused, but they were encouraged to promote an independent scheme, and in the autumn of 1844 the prospectus of the Cornwall Railway was produced. The line was to run from Plymouth, crossing the Hamoaze near Torpoint, and within three-quarters of a mile of St Germans, and then via Liskeard, near Bodmin and Lostwithiel, then Par and St Austell to Truro and Falmouth. The crossing of the Hamoaze, about 800 yards wide at that point, was a sticking-point; the House of Lords rejected a proposal for a train ferry, recommending that a more carefully planned scheme should be prepared, avoiding the need for a ferry across the Hamoaze.

Brunel, brought in as engineer, proposed a new route with a bridge crossing the River Tamar about 2 miles above Torpoint, with some slightly eased gradients in Cornwall, but otherwise generally following the same line. This new proposal was given royal assent on 3 August 1846. The company was to have a capital of £1,600,000, of which about 15 per cent was subscribed by the Great Western, Bristol & Exeter, and South Devon railway companies. The line to Falmouth started from a junction with the South Devon Railway Company near its Plymouth station, and included a number of branches.

A shortage of money in the financial depression of the 1850s inhibited progress and, following the failure of the contractor for the Tamar bridge in 1855, the company started undertaking the continuation of the work itself, under the supervision of Brunel's assistant, Robert Pearson Brereton. The huge undertaking proceeded slowly but steadily and was completed in 1859.

The line was opened from Plymouth to Truro for passenger trains on 4 May 1859, and goods trains started on 3 October 1859. Passenger trains were limited to 30mph throughout and goods trains to 15mph; due to the shortage of money, the rolling stock fleet was very small and the train service sparse, with correspondingly low income. However, by August 1861 the directors of the company recorded their pleasure that large volumes of fish, potatoes and broccoli had been carried from West Cornwall to Truro by the West Cornwall Railway, which had a line from Penzance to Truro; the West Cornwall line was a narrow-gauge line, and all goods had to be trans-shipped into different wagons at Truro due to the break of gauge there.

The directors wished to extend their line to Falmouth, the original objective of the line, but money was still very difficult to obtain. The Associated Companies were forthcoming in return for a thousand-year lease of the line, an arrangement that was authorized by Act of Parliament in 1861.

A new start was made on constructing the Falmouth extension, and it opened to passenger services on 24 August 1863 (and for goods trains on 5 October). A new dock had been opened at Falmouth since the original plans for the railway and, despite the decline in the significance of Falmouth Docks to the railway company, an extension to that location was made, and a connection to the Dock Company's own rail network was made in January 1864.

A branch line to St Ives from St Erth (1877) heralded the start of a new era and developed an obscure little fishing village into a popular resort – a significant part of the Great Western's plan to bring tourism to the West Country. Soon visitors in their thousands were taking the branch line train from St Erth, and artists and writers were quick to respond to its charms, with Virginia Woolf's novel *To the Lighthouse* (1927) inspired by the town of St Ives.

The arrival of the railway stimulated urban growth everywhere, creating new classes of traveller – the commuter and the day-tripper – by enabling people to live away from their place of work and to take

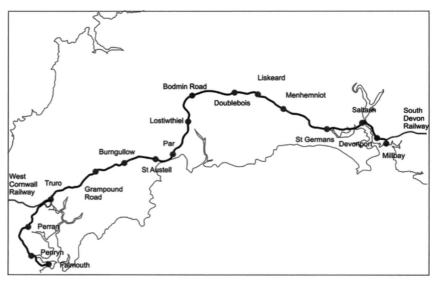

Map of Cornwall railway, showing stations when the line was opened to Falmouth in 1864.

holidays away from home. The railways, more than any other single factor, were also responsible for the development of most nineteenth-century seaside resorts. Places like St Ives, Falmouth and Newquay were revived with the arrival of the railway, while other towns were almost non-existent before the arrival of the railway. Almost every rail-head on the coast witnessed intense development around the terminus.

### 4.2.5 Digging deeper

Once the railways had been built, they needed locomotives and rolling stock, and workers to operate them. By 1900 over 620,000 people – nearly 5 per cent of the population – worked for the railways. The National Railway Museum in York has an excellent archive and library collection which holds letters, technical reports, engineering drawings, records of individuals and families, drivers' diaries, logbooks and much more. Trade Union archives are mainly housed at the University of Warwick's Modern Records Centre. There is also a Railway Ancestors Family History Society (www.railwayancestors.org.uk), which publishes magazines, periodicals and books on the subject, as well as providing a research service.

Di Drummond provides an accessible guide to *Tracing Your Railway Ancestors* with her publication through Pen & Sword Books.

The Railways Archive website (www.railwaysarchive.co.uk) provides access to nearly 4,000 documents on 9,000 accidents on the tracks, with links to related newspaper stories. Ancestry has digitized railway employment records from 1833 to 1963, although these do not include Great Western Railway records.

The Railways in the Nineteenth Century website, although aimed at schools, offers an impressive survey of British railway history from 1700 to 1900; it includes biographies of engineers, information about technological developments and details of railway towns.

### 4.2.6 Hidden treasures

As road transport increased, the branch line railways began to lose money, and it was perhaps inevitable that they would begin to close. Many were closed wholesale in the mid-1960s. Today, some remain successful in a variety of ways, while others can barely be traced, their tracks removed and their cuttings and embankments obliterated. In between is a range of lines, some still part of the national rail network, some industrial and some preserved as tourist and enthusiast attractions.

There are few relics left to remind people of the presence and importance of the railways. Viaducts, made of stone or concrete, which carried the trains across the valleys of the West Country, still remain as

Holsworthy 'Old' (or East) Viaduct in 1911 on the final approach to Holsworthy station in north Devon. Built in 1878 of local stone, the viaduct rises some 90ft above the valley floor.

monuments to both the construction of the railway and as lasting memorials.

Accidents, miraculous escapes and near-misses on the lines were often reported in local newspapers. One such accident occurred at Norton Fitzwarren in Somerset on 11 November 1890. In a report published by the Board of Trade on 15 November 1890, Lieutenant Colonel F.H. Rich stated:

> A special train, which consisted of a tank-engine, running funnel in front, two eight-wheeled composite carriages, and a brake-van with the guard at the tail of the train, ran at full speed into a down goods train, which had been placed on the up line on the Taunton side of Norton Fitzwarren station. Ten passengers in the front coach were killed, and nine others, as well as the driver and fireman of the special train were seriously injured. The guard of the train was also hurt, but not seriously.

Stones, plaques and other memorials are evident in local communities and in isolated locations, commemorating the railways of the West Country, the people who worked on the tracks and those who lost their lives on the lines.

Newspapers often report accidents on the lines. The *Western Daily Press* reported a fatal accident at Bristol railway station in its publication of Tuesday, 26 January 1869: 'Yesterday morning Edward Musty aged 45

Accident at Norton Fitzwarren, 1890.

and living at Charfield was run over by an engine that was being shunted at Bristol goods station of the Midland Railway. The wheels passed over his thighs and body mangling them fearfully. He was taken to the infirmary where he died in the course of the afternoon.' The following day a more detailed account of the accident was published and at the subsequent inquest, after hearing from witnesses, 'the jury … were of the opinion that no blame was attributable to anyone and they returned a verdict of Accidental Death'.

## 4.3 Inland waterways

For centuries rivers were used to transport goods and people around the country, with the mouths of different rivers linked by craft capable of passing along the coast. By 1660 there were 1,100 kilometres (685 miles) of navigable river in the United Kingdom. Later improvements to other rivers, including the Avon, the Kennet and the Wey in the south, meant that an additional 500 miles were added by 1724. Where rivers were straightened they became known as 'navigations' and although they were seen as the precursors to the canals, they remained rivers.

The earliest example of what we now regard as an artificial waterway was the Exeter Canal. Built between 1563 and 1566, it stretched almost 2 miles from the city to just below the Countess Weir and ran alongside the River Exe. However, it was not without its limitations; with a depth of 3 feet and a top width of 16, it could only take craft up to 16 tons. Very few seafaring vessels at this time were as small as this and so cargoes had to be trans-shipped into barges to reach Exeter by water.

### 4.3.1 The City of Bristol

The River Avon between Bath and Bristol was made navigable between 1724 and 1727, despite opposition from colliers and hauliers who feared the loss of their trade, though it was not until 1779 that a canal was substituted for the original proposal to deepen the river. In 1792 Bristol had been the focus of no fewer than three canal ventures – one from Bristol to Gloucester, another from Bristol to Taunton and a third linking Bristol with Southampton and London. That none came to anything was partly the result of the war against Napoleon, which was proving to be a drain on both money and the men needed to build the canals.

### 4.3.2 Somerset

One of the greatest unfulfilled canal schemes was the building of a waterway linking Bristol to Exeter. There were various late eighteenth-

and early nineteenth-century proposals and, although the through route remained a dream, a number of canals were built as independent parts of it. The Bridgwater & Taunton Canal is one such part, a 14-mile waterway that took nearly twenty years to construct. Finally completed in 1841, the canal, originally conceived as part of a much larger Bristol to Taunton waterway, was in the end little better than a more convenient alternative to the existing Tone and Parrett river navigations that already linked Bridgwater with Taunton. However, it did have one successful feature: a dock complex at Bridgwater which, from the 1840s, was a busy coal port often filled with trading schooners. The docks long outlived the canal, which fell into disuse in the early twentieth century.

The county of Somerset had two other notable waterways: the Chard Canal and the extravagantly named Grand Western Canal. The 13½-mile route from Creech St Michael to Chard was expensive and heavily engineered with three tunnels, two aqueducts and four inclined planes. Opened in 1842, it was closed by 1867, having been one of the least successful of all Britain's waterways and a total loss for its promoters. Surprisingly, much of its route can still be traced and its engineering features explored.

The Grand Western Canal was planned by John Rennie in the late eighteenth century as a waterway to link the River Tone in Taunton with the River Exe in Topsham, Devon. In 1816 the branch to Tiverton was opened and this was extended in 1838 to Taunton. No more of the Grand Western was ever built and those parts which were completed were overtaken by the railways within ten years.

### 4.3.3 Devon

The Exeter Ship Canal was the first canal in Britain to be built with locks. It was deepened and enlarged between 1699 and 1701, to take seagoing craft up to 150 tons. This made Exeter a port again, and allowed West Country woollens to be shipped direct from the city and coal to be delivered to the city wharf. Subsequent improvements in 1830 admitted ships of up to 400 tons and for some years the canal saw a dynamic trade. The opening of the railway to Exeter in 1844 began a marked decline as small sailing vessels were driven off the seas by steamers too large for the canal. Exeter Corporation, the canal's owners, kept it open as a public utility and the Exeter Canal is therefore the only one in Devon to remain in use.

The Tavistock Canal opened in 1817 and was another remarkable piece of engineering. Its main line, just 4 miles long, included a tunnel through Morwelldown nearly 1½ miles in length, an aqueduct over the Lumburn river and an inclined plane with a fall of 237ft to connect with the Tamar. It was built with a slight downward gradient to provide a current for driving the mill and mining machinery on its course, and this also helped the heavily laden downward traffic. The 2-mile branch to the Mill Hill Quarries was opened in 1819 with wheeled cradles pulled by horsepower.

After the Napoleonic Wars the quarry and mining business proved much less profitable than had originally been expected. The Mill Hill branch of the Tavistock Canal fell into disuse in 1830 and, after the railway reached Tavistock in 1859, canal trade fell rapidly. The Duke of Bedford bought the canal for one-twentieth of what the canal had cost in 1873 and trade ceased. However, in 1934 the canal channel was cleaned and its current output re-employed to drive a hydro-electric plant in Morwellham.

In the north of the county Torrington Canal was privately financed by the Rolle family. Opening in 1827, it transported sand and lime from the estuary of the River Torridge, near Bideford, 6 miles inland to Torrington, and served farms along the way. It was closed in 1871 and much of it has disappeared, with only its main feature, a most impressive five-arched stone aqueduct, built to take the canal across the Torridge, still surviving. It now carries the driveway to the local mansion, Beam House, with part of the canal line being used for the railway.

### 4.3.4 Cornwall

Agricultural demands inspired the construction of many canals in the West Country as sea sand was used as a fertiliser. There were only five canal schemes in Cornwall, with one dating back to the eighteenth century. The half-mile-long Parnall's Canal was built in about 1720 near St Austell. It was closed due to a rock slide in about 1732 and is referred to very briefly in Charles Hadfield's publication, *The Canals of Southwest England*.

The most ambitious tub-boat canal scheme was the Bude Canal, built by James Green under an act of 1819 and completed in 1825, to transport sand from Bude to the villages and farms around Holsworthy and the Tamar. The tub-boats, small square barges, were moved by horses in trains of up to six, and they were fitted with wheels to allow them to be drawn up the six inclined planes on rails. The trade never reached anything like the expected volume, although the company did manage to keep solvent until the appearance of railway competition. The railway reached Launceston in 1865 and Holsworthy in 1879, and by 1880 the canal tolls could no longer cover the running costs. In 1891 the main Druxton to Blagdonmoor Wharf line was closed but the branch from Alfardisworthy Reservoir to Bude remained open to supply water to Bude.

There were a few abortive canal schemes in Cornwall, including the St Columb Canal, sometimes referred to as Edyvean's Canal. Authorized in 1773, the scheme was certainly not short of funds as the Cornish engineer John Edyvean, who first proposed the canal, appears to have spent most of his own fortune and his sister's money as well before realizing that he was unlikely to recoup much of it and abandoning the project. In 1829 Richard Retallick, a businessman from Liskeard, revived the idea of a canal from St Columb to Mawgan Porth, and issued a prospectus which was part of a larger project to make Porth suitable for use as a harbour. However, no further progress was made on this canal.

### 4.3.5 Digging deeper

No one made a fortune from canals in the West Country. In fact, most people who invested lost heavily. Before the railways came, however, they were a useful means of transport and were of much more value to the districts they served than to their owners.

Accessible guides to British canals at a national level have been written by Nick Corble, detailing the history of the waterways with a wealth of colour illustrations. Anthony Burton and Derek Pratt also produced several publications on *The Anatomy of Canals* from the early years, through mania years to decline and renewal. Other materials are available, specific to particular canals, and several are noted in the references for this chapter.

The passage of the private Acts of Parliament that authorized the canals can be followed in the House of Commons and House of Lords Journals, where the sponsors of local canals and any opposition are noted. The National Archives contains papers and correspondence relating to individual canals, including a large amount of information on proposed closures, under MT 52 and MT 63. Local record offices have minute books, correspondence and engineers' reports, as well as other documents relating to the canal schemes of the eighteenth and nineteenth centuries.

Ordnance Survey maps also provide an excellent aid to discovering obscure canal routes and waterways.

The Rolle Aqueduct, Torrington, Devon (1950s).

### 4.3.6 Hidden treasures

A random collection of over a thousand original maps and plans of canals and inland river navigations are available on the Canal Maps Archive website (www.canalmaps.net). Dating from 1677 to the present day, there are many examples from the 'canal age' (1760–1830), both manuscript and printed.

Aqueducts from the canal mania era are still evident, with many offering an alternative to their original purpose when built. Some of the canal towpaths and trails are now used as tourist attractions, featuring sights such as the mileposts which enabled boatmen and canal companies to calculate precisely how far boats had journeyed, and markers which indicated the original land-ownership boundaries. Some of the waterways are still navigable by barge, including the Bridgwater & Taunton Canal in Somerset and the Grand Western Canal in Devon, with many of them entrusted into the care of the Canal and River Trust.

*Chapter 5*

# LOCAL GOVERNMENT

In *The Oxford Companion to Local and Family History*, David Hey opens the entry on this subject by stating that it 'has a reputation for dullness', though he does go on to say that 'some understanding of the evolution of local government is essential … for what it can tell us about the concerns and aspirations of individual communities'.

## 5.1 An overview of local government

The feudal system introduced by the Normans was designed to govern rural areas which could easily be controlled by a lord. Since the system was based upon the exploitation of the labour and produce of peasant farmers, it was unsuited to governing larger towns, where more complex economic activity was required. At the time of the Norman Conquest there were few true urban centres in England, but during the early medieval period a growing population and increased mercantile activity led to an increase in the importance of towns.

It was Henry II who greatly enhanced the separation of towns from the countryside, granting around 150 royal charters to towns in England, which were thereafter referred to as 'boroughs'. For an annual rent to the Crown, the towns were given various privileges, such as exemption from feudal dues, the right to hold a market and the right to levy certain taxes. However, not all market towns established during this period were self-governing.

The self-governing boroughs are the first noticeably modern aspect of local government in England. Generally they were run by a town corporation, made up of a council of aldermen, the town 'elders'. Although each corporation was different, they were usually self-elected, new members being co-opted by the existing members. A mayor was often elected by the council to serve for a given period. The idea of a town council to run the affairs of an individual town remains an important part of local government in England today.

In the 1540s the office of Lord Lieutenant was instituted in each county, replacing the feudal lords as the Crown's direct representative in that county. The lieutenants had a military role, previously exercised by the sheriffs, and were made responsible for raising and organizing the county militia. The county lieutenancies were subsequently given responsibility for the Volunteer Force.

From the sixteenth century the county was increasingly used as a unit of local government. Although 'small government' was still the accepted norm, there were an increasing number of responsibilities that could not be fulfilled by individual communities. The justices of the peace therefore took on various administrative functions known as 'county business'. This was conducted at the quarter sessions, assembled four times a year by the Lord Lieutenant. In 1871 the lieutenants lost their positions as head of the militias, and the office became largely ceremonial.

By the nineteenth century the county magistrates exercised powers over the licensing of alehouses, construction of bridges, prisons and asylums, superintendence of main roads, public buildings and charitable institutions, and regulation of weights and measures. The justices were empowered to levy local taxes to support these activities, and in 1739 these were unified as a single 'county rate' under the control of a county treasurer. In order to build and maintain roads and bridges, a salaried county surveyor was to be appointed.

These county functions were attached to the legal system, since this was the only body which acted county-wide at that time. However, in this ad hoc system the beginnings of county councils, another central element in modern local government, can be observed. The counties themselves remained more or less static between the Law in Wales Acts of 1535–42, and the Great Reform Act of 1832.

The ecclesiastical parishes of the Church of England also came to play *de jure* roles in local government from this time with people of rural communities taking care of whatever local administration was required. Although the parishes were in no sense governmental organizations, laws were passed requiring parishes to carry out certain responsibilities. From 1555 parishes were responsible for the upkeep of local roads. From 1605 parishes administered the Poor Law, and were required to collect money for their own poor. The parishes were run by parish councils, known as 'vestries', sometimes elected from among the rate-payers, but often self-selecting.

## 5.2  The Poor Law

British social policy was dominated by the Poor Laws, first passed in 1598 and continuing until 1948. The Elizabethan Poor Law of 1601 provided for a compulsory poor rate, the creation of 'overseers' of relief and a provision for 'setting the poor on work'. The parish was the basic unit of administration. There was, however, no general mechanism through which this could be enforced, and the operation of the Poor Law was inconsistent between areas.

During the Industrial Revolution there were vast increases in population, particularly in urban areas, and this resulted in the genesis of an urban poor, who had no means of subsistence. This created many new problems with which the small-scale local government apparatus existing in England was unable to cope. Between 1832 and 1888 several laws were passed in an attempt to address these problems. The first was the Poor Law Amendment Act of 1834 which emphasized two principles: (1) less eligibility: the position of the pauper must be 'less eligible' than that of the labourer; and (2) the workhouse test: no relief outside the workhouse. This Act took the responsibility for the management of the Poor Law out of the hands of parishes and placed it in the hands of Poor Law Unions managed by an elected Board of Guardians, composed of magisterial and elected members, with salaried overseers. Each of these boards was responsible to the Poor Law Commission. A further Act in 1835, the Municipal Incorporation Act, obliged boroughs to organize police forces under the supervision of elected watch committees and not the magistracy. This was extended by the Rural Constabulary Act of 1839, allowing the magistrates to establish rural police forces under their own supervision, while a further statute of 1842 permitted parishes to employ paid constables to supplement parish resources. However, making policing dependent upon the decisions of the unelected elite was clearly unsatisfactory and this led to a further statute in 1856 which called for the existence of a uniformed police force.

The Poor Laws were much hated, and a large number of the developments of social services in the twentieth century – including national insurance, means tests and health care – were framed to avoid having to rely on them.

## 5.3  Reform acts of the nineteenth century

The development of modern government in England in general began with the Great Reform Act of 1832. The impetus for this act was provided by corrupt practices in the House of Commons, as well as the massive increases in population which occurred during the Industrial Revolution. Boroughs and counties sent two representatives to the House of Commons. Theoretically, the honour of electing Members of Parliament belonged to the wealthiest and most flourishing towns in the kingdom. Boroughs that ceased to be successful could be disenfranchised by the Crown. In practice, however, many tiny hamlets became boroughs, especially between the reigns of Henry VIII and Charles II. Likewise, boroughs that had flourished during the Middle Ages but had since fallen into decay were allowed to continue sending representatives to Parliament. These were known as 'rotten boroughs'.

The Great Reform Act disenfranchised the rotten boroughs, and redistributed representation in Parliament to the centres of population. It also enfranchised those in the lower social and economic scale, as the act extended the right to vote to any man owning a household worth £10, adding 217,000 voters to an electorate of 435,000. Approximately one man in five now had the right to vote.

A further Reform Act in 1867 extended the right to vote still further down the class ladder, adding just short of a million voters and doubling the electorate to almost two million in England and Wales. This created major shock-waves in contemporary British culture, some of which are reflected in works such as Arnold's *Culture and Anarchy* and Ruskin's *Crown of Wild Olive*, as authors debated whether this shift of power would create a democracy that would, in turn, destroy high culture.

The 1884 Bill and the 1885 Redistribution Act tripled the electorate, giving the vote to most agricultural labourers. By this time voting was becoming a right rather than the property of the privileged. However, it is worth noting that women were not granted voting rights until the Act of 1918, which enfranchised all men over 21 and women over 30. This final piece of discrimination was eliminated ten years later, in 1928, by the Equal Franchise Act.

## 5.4 The Duchy of Cornwall

The duchy was established in 1337 out of the former earldom of Cornwall by Edward III for his son, Edward, Prince of Wales, the 'Black Prince', who became the first Duke of Cornwall. The duchy consisted of two parts: the title and honour, and the landed estate that supported it financially. The core of the estate at its foundation was the seventeen duchy manors found within the county. However, the duchy does not share the same boundaries as the county, and much of the estate has always been outside those boundaries. That said, the duchy maintains a special relationship with Cornwall, and maintains various rights, such as that of appointing the county's High Sheriff. The extent of the estate has varied as holdings have been sold and acquired over the years, both within Cornwall and in other counties.

The duchy owns 54,090 hectares of land (around 133,658 acres) over twenty-three counties, with nearly half of the holdings in Devon, and other large assets in Cornwall, Herefordshire, Somerset and Wales. These include farming, residential and commercial properties, as well as an investment portfolio. In modern times the considerable revenue from the duchy has been the primary source of income for the Prince of Wales.

The duchy was created with the express purpose of providing income to the heir apparent to the throne; thus, it traditionally goes to the eldest son of the reigning monarch. Although the duke owns the income from the estate, he does not own the estate outright and does not have the right to sell capital assets for his own benefit. The duke owns freehold about three-fifths of the Cornish foreshore and the 'fundus', or bed, of navigable rivers and has right of wreck on all ships wrecked on Cornish shores, including those afloat offshore, and also to 'royal fish', i.e. whales, porpoises and sturgeon.

It is also worth noting that both the Duchy of Cornwall and the Duchy of Lancaster have special legal rights not available to other landed estates: for example, the rules on *bona vacantia*, the right to ownerless property, operate in favour of the holders of the duchies rather than the Crown, such that the property of anyone who dies in the county of Cornwall without a will or identifiable heirs, and assets belonging to dissolved companies whose registered office was in Cornwall, pass to the duchy.

## 5.5 Justices of the Peace

The role of Justices of the Peace (JPs) was developed from the 'Keepers of the Peace', who were appointed by a commission in the thirteenth century. They were given the power to try minor offenders by a statute in 1361, when they acquired their name, and in the fourteenth and fifteenth centuries were appointed by the Crown from the ranks of the major land-owners. Justices of the Peace received no payment for their duties and were expected to enforce the principal statutes concerning the peace, to take financial guarantees for good behaviour, and to imprison those who would or could not provide this surety. Serious crimes were tried at the assizes.

In Tudor times the duties of JPs were greatly extended and by the end of Elizabeth I's reign 309 statutes had imposed responsibilities of either a judicial or administrative nature. In effect, the JPs were the rulers of the counties of England from the Elizabethan period onwards, successfully adapting to the changing requirements over the centuries. In 1888 they began to lose their powers when their administrative functions were transferred to elected councils in each county and large town. Responsibility for the police was divided between the JPs and the new councils, and quarter sessions continued to sit as criminal courts until 1971, with the modern magistrates' courts evolving from this ancient system.

## 5.6 Criminality
Courts of summary jurisdiction held by two or more Justices of the Peace or magistrates for trying lesser offences or to enquire into indictable offences were known as petty sessions. The proceedings of the seventeenth- and eighteenth-century sessions are not well recorded. The system of quarterly meetings of the Justices of the Peace for each county and county borough began in 1361 to enforce law and order, conformity to religion, the regulation of trade, commerce and employment, the maintenance of the poor and the upkeep of roads and bridges. The Courts of Assizes tried capital and other offences such as larceny, arson, burglary, rape, robbery and homicide, which were too serious to be tried at quarter sessions. The assize judges also tried a variety of civil cases.

The assize circuits that remained in use until 1876 had been defined in the fourteenth century. England was divided into six circuits beyond London and Middlesex; the Western circuit covered the counties of Somerset, Devon and Cornwall, while Bristol was covered by the Oxford circuit.

## 5.7 Prisons and transportation
The history of prisons in Britain (other than dungeons in castles and other holding locations) began in the sixteenth century with the London Bridewell. Although there were earlier gaols, the houses of correction were the first organized nationwide gaols. They were local, controlled by the JPs and panels of other dignitaries, and were mainly for a mix of debtors and remand prisoners. Convicted prisoners could also be housed but were more often hanged or transported (or sent to the hulks to await transportation).

The West Country's most infamous prison is Dartmoor Prison. In the heart of Dartmoor, in the village of Princetown, the prison was originally built to house Napoleonic prisoners of war, alleviating the potentially disastrous situation of thousands of French prisoners being held on hulk ships in Plymouth, with an arsenal of weapons not far away. When the last prisoner left Dartmoor in 1816, the prison was wound down. In the wider world, the colonies to which our convicts were being transported were becoming fastidious about the company they kept, with all, except Western Australia, closing their doors to convicts by 1846. The situation in Britain was becoming desperate. Ninety prisons were built between 1842 and 1877, and Dartmoor Prison reopened in 1850 as a civilian prison. In 1917 it was converted into a Home Office Work Centre for certain conscientious objectors granted release from prison, and reopened as a prison in 1920 for Britain's most serious offenders. Over the years Dartmoor Prison has seen many an escapee, and indeed a mutiny in 1932. Now a Category C prison, HMP Dartmoor houses mainly non-violent offenders and white-collar criminals.

There are four other prisons in the West Country which remain open: HMP Exeter, HMP Channings Wood, HMP Shepton Mallet in Somerset (sometimes known as Cornhill), and HMP Bristol, previously known as Horfield Prison, a male adults and young offenders' prison.

HMP Exeter accepts all male adults and young offenders committed to prison by the courts from Cornwall, Devon and West Somerset, while HMP Channings Wood houses offenders serving a wide range of sentence lengths, and predominantly receives new arrivals from local prisons across the West Country. Two of the residential living blocks at the prison make up the Vulnerable Prisoners Unit, which specializes in delivering Sex Offender Treatment Programmes.

HMP Shepton Mallet was established as a House of Correction in 1625, to comply with an act of King James I in 1609 requiring that every county had such a house. In the seventeenth century Shepton Mallet was not the only place of imprisonment in Somerset: the County Gaol was in Ilchester, and there was another House of Correction at Ilchester and another at Taunton. The United Kingdom's oldest operating prison, Shepton Mallet served an important role in the Second World War when, following its closure in 1930, it was reopened for military use. The prison took into protective storage many important historical documents from the Public Record Office in London, including the Magna Carta, the Domesday Book, the logbooks of HMS *Victory*, the Olive Branch Petition (1775), dispatches from the Battle of Waterloo and the 'scrap of paper' signed by Hitler and Prime Minister Neville Chamberlain at the Munich Conference of September 1938. In all, about 300 tons of records were transported to Shepton Mallet. Having returned to civilian use in 1966, Shepton Mallet is now a Category C Lifer Prison.

Cornwall also has a historic jail at Bodmin, which was built in 1779 by prisoners of war. During its 150 years of operation, it saw over fifty public hangings. The Debtors Act of 1869 abolished imprisonment for debt so the prison had spare space that was taken over by the Admiralty for naval prisoners. Eventually, the naval prison occupied an entire wing of the building, before it was closed in 1922.

## 5.8 Digging deeper

All the record offices have lists of surviving parish records, as well as indexes of certain groups of records, most notably the Poor Law records, and these will be covered in depth in Chapter 11. The history of local government in its heroic days of urban poverty, destitution and disease in industrialized society is now well described in both fictional literature and written histories. However, the history of the other provisions within the local communities is less well known, and this provides fertile ground for the family and local historian, with publications such as Keith-Lucas's *English Local Government in the Nineteenth and Twentieth Centuries*, Landau's *The Justices of the Peace 1679–1760* and S. and B. Webb's *The Parish and the County* and *The Manor and the Borough* providing an excellent basis for research.

County record offices and local studies libraries hold borough and corporation archives dating back to before the nineteenth-century Reform Acts. Poll books for county elections, first published in 1696, are generally divided by parish, with the name of each voter listed and who they voted for, compiled by the sheriff. These continued until 1872, when the secret ballot was introduced, and the poll books became superfluous. The Guildhall Library in London holds a large collection of poll books for the whole of England and the Society of Genealogists also has many directories and poll books in their library, a list of which can be found in their suitably titled publication, *Directories & poll books, including almanacs & electoral rolls, in the Library of the Society of Genealogists* (1995). Relatively few poll books survive for Devon and those that do are normally listed in the catalogues of the main local studies collections, as well as online at The Genealogist and Findmypast. Some are available at the Society of Genealogists, with a few catalogues published by S&N Genealogy Supplies. It is worth consulting R. Gwyn Thomas's article entitled 'An "Unknown" Devon County Poll-Book' in the *Transactions of the Devonshire Association*, which provides an account of the 1712 election, the only parliamentary contest for the county constituency before 1790, and a transcript of the surviving poll books.

For Cornwall, there are three poll books, all held by the Cornwall Record Office: 1710 (CF4787), 1774 (DX622), and 1790 (PD208), with some extracts available online. Somerset poll books are located at the Somerset Heritage Centre, with transcripts available for particular areas of the county. The City of Bristol poll book of 1830 has been fully scanned and is available to purchase on CD as well as on microfilm through the Family History Centres of the Church of Jesus Christ of Latter-day Saints (LDS). A nationwide guide to holdings is provided in *Poll books c. 1696–1872* by Jeremy Gibson.

Many county record offices and libraries have copies of electoral registers relating to the region. The British Library holds a national set from 1918 onwards and Findmypast is due to make them available in 2013. A comprehensive listing is provided in Gibson and Rogers' *Electoral Registers since 1832*. It is worth noting that it is challenging to obtain access to the most recent electoral registers.

Some protestation returns from 1641/2 are retained by local studies libraries and county record offices. The West Country Studies Library in Exeter holds transcripts by A.J. Howard, published in 1973, and copies of various returns for the county of Devon have been made available on the Devon Heritage website in its history section.

Surviving quarter-sessions records dating from the sixteenth and seventeenth centuries may be consulted at county record offices, and online indexes are available via the Access to Archives website. Most counties have a series of indictment and order books, which record the cases under discussion and the decisions that were made. Where they survive, informal papers such as petitions and depositions provide much more human detail: for example, the petition at Devon Quarter Sessions, 15 July 1755, relating to the Holbeton fire on 16 September 1754 (extracted from QS 1/19, pp. 237–8), in which petitioners sought permission to raise a charitable appeal for help after losing their homes and possessions after a disastrous fire. Named in the record as having suffered losses are Ann and Honor Algar, Richard Berry, James and Ralph Hingston, John Husk, William Lake, Susanna Langley, William Macy, William Pike, Andrew Popplestone, and Andrew and John Tarring, while James Algar and Francis Burrows are named as local builders.

Many records of the assize courts are held at the National Archives (under ASSI 21–30, covering the period 1610–1971 for the Western Circuit), but they are among the most difficult to use for the purposes of family and local history and the records are poorly preserved. The National Archives finding aid entitled *English criminal trials 1559–1971 –*

*a key to assize records* provides a detailed reference guide to the series relating to each county's Crown and Gaol books, indictments, depositions and any other records held.

Although the vast majority of assize records are kept at the National Archives, a small number of relevant records are held in county record offices, with Bristol assizes records prior to 1832 held at Bristol Record Office. Contemporary newspapers or pamphlets often reported local cases in much detail. To find out about surviving newspapers and to view them, use the British Newspaper Archive or contact the appropriate local county record office.

The Old Bailey Online website provides detailed proceedings (although not complete transcripts of what was said) in trials at the London Central Criminal Court.

John Howard's *The State of the Prisons* was published in 1777, and substantial reports were written throughout the eighteenth and nineteenth centuries. There are numerous excellent publications about prisons, the prison system and how to trace your criminal ancestors, which are referenced in the bibliography for this chapter.

Many authors have been captivated by the subject of Dartmoor Prison, with books by Simon Dell, Trevor James, Ron Joy and Elizabeth Stanbrook, as well as numerous others, providing a fascinating insight into the 200-year history of the prison. *Bodmin 1901–2000: A Century of Memories* includes a section on Bodmin Gaol, with excerpts from the *Cornish Guardian*.

Prison hulk registers and letter books in England (1802–1849) are searchable by name at the National Archives (HO 9) and have been digitized and made available on the Ancestry and Findmypast websites. These registers contain personal information on the prisoners, and where and when they were convicted. Licences of parole issued to female convicts (PCOM 4) are also available on the Ancestry website; their content is variable, but they can include a variety of personal details, reports on behaviour while in prison and, from 1871, photographs. The *Looking for records of a prisoner* finding aid on the National Archives website provides further details on records held and further documentation is available on Documents Online.

The Convict Transportation Registers Database (1787–1867) has been compiled from the British Home Office (HO) records which are available on microfilm at all Australian State Libraries, with the names, term of years, transport ships and other details for over 123,000 of the estimated 160,000 convicts transported to Australia in the eighteenth and nineteenth centuries available online.

## 5.9 Hidden treasures

There are very few attractions, museums or heritage centres which focus on the day-to-day workings of local government, apart from those which are devoted to gaol history. Dartmoor Prison Museum and Visitor Centre holds an interesting collection of artefacts and provides a unique insight into prison life past and present. Bodmin Jail, a unique heritage asset, is open to the public, with a fascinating museum of Cornish penal life over the last three centuries. The present owners, who acquired it in 2004, are reviving the gaol by replacing the roofs and internal structures, and showing the cells as they once were.

## Chapter 6

# ARMY AND NAVY HISTORY

One way or another, war and conquest (or the prospect of either) played a substantial role in the lives of our forebears. From William the Conqueror to the present day, the people of the West Country have been affected by all national and international conflicts, and in many cases their landscape and local communities have been significantly altered as a result. Over the centuries, the impact of wars and conflicts can be seen throughout the West Country with war memorials commemorating those who lost their lives fighting for our country.

In the seventeenth century the English Civil War (1642–1646) tore England apart. At the heart of the conflict lay the policies and personality of King Charles I and his apparent determination to rule England without the assistance of Parliament. All counties of the West Country saw bloody battles, with Cornwall playing a significant role as a Royalist enclave in the generally Parliamentarian south-west. The Devon town of Torrington was the site of one of the last major battles of the war on the night of 16 February 1646, the outcome of which helped to bring about the demise of royalist power in England.

Led by General Thomas Fairfax, the Parliamentarian New Model Army swept into the town under cover of darkness and fought a fierce battle with Lord Hopton's Royalist forces. The skirmish involved approximately 17,000 men on foot and on horseback, who fought in the streets of Torrington. As the battle proceeded, a stray spark ignited the Royalists' powder magazine stored in Torrington Church. Eighty barrels of gunpowder exploded, blowing the roof off the church and killing many Royalist soldiers and Parliamentarian prisoners in and around the church. The explosion effectively ended the battle. In the resulting confusion, Lord Hopton and what remained of the Royalist Western Army withdrew from Torrington and escaped into Cornwall. Lord Hopton surrendered to Fairfax at Truro on 14 March 1646, agreeing to disband the Western Army and to go into exile. The battle at Torrington marked the end of Royalist resistance in the West Country and led to the eventual defeat and execution of King Charles I.

During the wars of the eighteenth and nineteenth centuries, in particular those of the French Revolution and Napoleon, Plymouth was a vital base for the blockade of the opposing French coast and ports, and the town saw significant improvements to its fortifications. These wars brought so many prizes that the vast number of prisoners became an embarrassment, with thousands of them housed in hulk ships moored in the Hamoaze and in the Millbay Prison.

The army and navy represented a major source of employment for many of our forebears, and the distribution of the population was greatly affected by the migration of our ancestors and their families to naval bases and army barracks, with a burgeoning population in these areas. Many people's ancestors served in either the Royal Navy or the army, and these individuals are often of special research interest. Army and navy records provide fascinating information about an ancestor's life and any wars in which he took part, and frequently contain vital genealogical information.

## 6.1 The militia

The obligation to serve in the militia in England derives from a common law tradition dating back to Anglo-Saxon times that all able-bodied males were liable to be called out to serve as a local defence force, either to preserve internal order or to defend the locality against an invader. The procedures for raising the militia were set out by an Act of 1757, and from time to time constables were ordered to draw up lists of all the men of a certain age within their parishes who were able to serve. Initially the age bracket was between 18 and 50 but the upper limit was reduced to 45 in 1762.

A ballot was then held to decide which of them should be called upon to serve, or else pay for a replacement. Certain members of the community were excused from service, including peers, clergymen, constables, apprentices, seamen, soldiers and those who had previously served. In some ballots judges, medical practitioners and licensed teachers were also excused.

From 1758 most lists include the man's occupation; from 1802, how many children the man had; and from 1806, the man's age. The system was organized by the Lord Lieutenants of each county, the Justices of the Peace and the parish constables.

## 6.2 Digging deeper

The location of muster rolls, together with details either of the militia's income or what arms they were supposed to provide, is given in William Spencer's *Records of the Militia and Volunteer Forces*. The earliest rolls survive from the sixteenth century, particularly the period 1522–1640, with most records held at the National Archives or online at Findmypast. Records of militia men held at the National Archives include WO 13 (1780–1878) and WO 68 (1859–1925) and there are a few birth and baptism records of serving militia men's children in WO 32 and WO 68.

Gibson and Dell's *Tudor and Stuart muster rolls, a directory of holdings in the British Isles* lists the rolls which have been published, including the Devon muster roll of 1569, with about 18,000 names.

## 6.3 Hidden treasures

The *Exeter Militia List 1803* lists George Sillifant in the parish of Exeter St David, aged 43 with two children, and required to provide a musket if called to defend his community. An act of 1758 required that all men of the relevant age, even those excused service, should be listed. This gives an insight into the residents within communities when censuses were little more than head counts.

## 6.4 The Royal Navy

The origins of Plymouth can be traced back to Saxon times, more than a thousand years ago, and its history very much reflects its maritime location. During the sixteenth to eighteenth centuries Plymouth established its reputation both as a centre for voyage and discovery, and

Exeter Militia list for St David, 1803.

| | SAINT DAVID | | | |
|---|---|---|---|---|
| William FORD | Nursery man | 28 | | Willing to serve |
| William SKINNER | Gardener | | 30 1 chd. | Do. |
| Edward BOWDEN | Vintner | | 41 2 chn. under 10 | Serving in the Cavalry |
| James WOOD | Ostler | | 53 | |
| John QUICK | Boots | 19 | | |
| William CULLUM | Printer | | 23 1 chd. | Enrolled to serve in the Rifle Corps |

for its military importance. This was generally considered to be due to its location, close to the Atlantic Ocean, and its large harbour. Transatlantic trade originated with William Hawkins in 1528, and his son John laid the foundations of an organized naval force. In 1572 Francis Drake became the first Englishman to sail into the Pacific, embarking on the first ever circumnavigation of the globe in 1577. Knighted by Elizabeth I in 1581, Sir Francis Drake masterminded the defeat of the Spanish Armada in 1588 from his Plymouth base.

The most celebrated expedition to leave Plymouth was that of the Pilgrim Fathers. Persecuted for their Puritan beliefs in eastern England, they set sail for the New World on board the *Mayflower* in 1620. After spending a few weeks in Provincetown at the tip of Cape Cod, they eventually landed in Plymouth Harbour, Massachusetts and helped to establish a new Plymouth community.

Plymouth's military expansion began in earnest in the late 1660s when the royal citadel was built on the highest point above the town, the Hoe (meaning high ground). It incorporated the old fort built in the time of Sir Francis Drake. In 1690 the first royal dockyard opened on the banks of the Tamar west of Plymouth. Further docks were built in 1727, 1762 and 1793, and a huge naval complex was later established, including the communities of Plymouth Dock and Stonehouse. The navy's role during war against Napoleon's France was pivotal, and in 1812 a mile-long breakwater was laid to protect the fleet.

Throughout the nineteenth century the population and physical size of the towns increased dramatically. In 1824 Plymouth Dock was renamed Devonport, with the three towns of Plymouth, Devonport and Stonehouse united as the Borough of Plymouth in 1914.

## 6.5 Digging deeper

There are many publications documenting the history of Plymouth Dock's expansion into Devonport royal dockyard, once one of the biggest naval bases in the country. One of particular note is Sylvia Guthrig's *From Plymouth Dock to Devonport*, published by the Devon Family History Society. The Cyber Heritage website also provides a vast amount of information about Plymouth's history, including photographs, videos, documents and historical resources.

Most naval records are held by the National Archives (ADM series), with records for a number of individual officers in the navy held in county record offices; for example, Devon Heritage Centre holds the mess book, letters, etc., of J.P.B. Chichester (1812–1828), the journal of Browne Smith, training as an officer (1824–1827), and the midshipman's journal of J.H.A. Stucley (1934–1936). A few sixteenth- and seventeenth-century documents, together with a list of Barnstaple men enrolled in the navy in 1795, are held in the Barnstaple Borough Collection, while the deeds for the navy yard in Barnstaple (1860–1870) form part of the Barnstaple Town Council deposit.

The Plymouth & West Devon Record Office has a large section on maritime history, including Royal Naval Commissions, certificates of service, correspondence, diaries and journals for the eighteenth to twentieth centuries, and their website provides details of their holdings with links to other websites on the subject.

Many men worked at the dockyard as clerks or tradesmen and their records are also in the ADM series at the National Archives, particularly pay books (ADM 42, 32, 36 and 37) and books containing physical descriptions of tradesmen between 1748 and 1830 (ADM 106).

Sailors who served from 1853 onwards can be easily traced through the indexed continuous service engagement books at the National Archives, or on their website, in AGM 139 (1853–1872) and ADM 188 (1873–1923). Providing date and place of birth and occupation before engagement, as well as other details such as age, height, hair colour, eye colour, complexion and any wounds, scars or marks of note, the Royal Navy Registers of Seamen's Services are often very detailed and offer the family historian a plethora of information to develop a greater knowledge of their ancestor.

An ambitious project to 'establish accurate biographical information on those individuals who have served, or supported the Royal Navy since 1660', the Naval Biographical Database is privately developed and

ADM 188/464/113 Royal Navy, Register of Seamen's Service at Devonport – George Phillifant, born 18 May 1877 in Lifton, Devon.

funded – a budding resource for those with an interest in the Royal Navy. This is not yet complete, and only contains information about officers between 1660 and 1815.

Entire chapters of family history publications are dedicated to the topic of the Royal Navy, including Anthony Adolph's *Tracing Your Family History*, the 'where to search' section of which is highly recommended, as is Simon Fowler's publication on the subject, *Tracing Your Naval Ancestors*.

## 6.6 Hidden treasures

The Fleet Air Arm Museum at Yeovilton has an extensive collection of military and civilian aircraft as well as models of Royal Navy ships, especially aircraft carriers.

The world's largest maritime museum, the National Maritime Museum at Greenwich in London, enables visitors to 'discover 500 years of Britain's encounter with the world at sea' with the National Maritime Museum Cornwall, located in Falmouth.

Devonport has its own Naval Base Museum with collections based on support to the fleet since the time of Edward I (r. 1272–1307), including archives and artefacts, and provides access to industrial buildings from the eighteenth and nineteenth centuries, ships and submarine tours.

## 6.7 The army

The army has its roots in the troops Charles II employed full-time after his Restoration in 1660, and whose numbers were dramatically expanded by James II (r. 1685–1688). Officers aside, few records exist prior to the eighteenth century. The army comprised regiments of foot soldiers and mounted cavalry, supplemented by special regiments such as the Royal Artillery, Royal Horse Artillery and Royal Engineers. In the Childers Reforms of 1881 the infantry was reorganised and most regiments were linked to a county.

The Somerset Light Infantry was an infantry regiment in the British Army. It was formed in 1685 as the Earl of Huntingdon's 13th Regiment of Foot. In 1782 the county name was included in the title and in 1881 the regiment became known as Prince Albert's Light Infantry (Somersetshire Regiment). The regiment saw action during the First and Second World Wars, and in India and Malaya, with terrible losses in the First World War in particular. In 1959 the regiment amalgamated with the Duke of Cornwall's Light Infantry (DCLI), created in 1881 by the merger of the 32nd (Cornwall Light Infantry) Regiment of Foot and the 46th (South Devonshire) Regiment of Foot, to become the Somerset and

Cornwall Light Infantry. It is now known as the Light Infantry, after being renamed again in 1988.

In June 1667 Henry Somerset, Marquess of Worcester, was granted a commission to raise a regiment of foot, the Marquess of Worcester's Regiment of Foot. The regiment remained in existence for only a few months and was disbanded in the same year. It was re-raised in January 1673 and again disbanded in 1674. In 1682 Henry Somerset was created Duke of Beaufort, and in 1685 he was again commissioned to raise a regiment, the Duke of Beaufort's Regiment of Foot, or the Beaufort Musketeers, to defend Bristol against the Duke of Monmouth's rebellion. The regiment served under the name of its various colonels until it was numbered as the 11th Regiment of Foot when the numerical system of regimental designation was adopted in 1751. It was given the additional county title of 11th (North Devonshire) Regiment of Foot in 1782. In 1881, under the Childers Reforms, it became the Devonshire Regiment, at the same time merging with the militia and rifle volunteer units of the county of Devon.

Each of the county's regiments was heavily involved in the First and Second World Wars, both of which had a devastating effect on so many families. In the First World War alone about a million men died and twice as many were wounded, this being borne out by most family trees.

## 6.8 Digging deeper

Many regiments have published regimental histories and maintain regimental museums which usually hold some records (but rarely personnel records), photographs, uniforms and other relevant material. The Army Museum Ogilvy Trust provides information on the location of military museums and the few regimental records which they hold – most museums in the West Country have passed their records to county record offices.

An online guide to regimental histories and engagements is available from the British Army website, under the British Army Structure section. *Tracing Your Army Ancestors* by Simon Fowler and *Family History in the Wars* by William Spencer are essential guides to all aspects of army research.

## 6.9 Hidden treasures

The National Army Museum and the Imperial War Museum, concerned with events after 1914, both contain splendid collections. The latter holds many photographic collections relating to the counties of the West Country, particularly of evacuees from Bristol to rural Devon and the

Women's Land Army training in Somerset in the Second World War, alongside uniforms and insignia for the West Country regiments.

Somerset has its own military museum, located in the twelfth-century great hall of Taunton Castle, which is part of the Museum of Somerset. Covering Somerset's military history from 1685 onwards, the museum has exhibitions on conflicts and on life in the regiments. Cornwall's Regimental Museum and regimental archives are housed in a listed Militia building built in Bodmin in 1859. The museum covers the history of the county regiment of Cornwall from the raising of the regiment in 1702 and the capture of Gibraltar in 1704, until its amalgamation in 1959. The Keep Military Museum in Dorchester in Dorset tells tales of the courage, humour and sacrifice of the soldiers and their families who have served in the regiments of Devon and Dorset for over 300 years.

# Chapter 7

# OCCUPATIONS

In 1066 much of the country was uninhabited, with large areas of land still given over to woodland. High moorlands were scarcely populated and the population of England was concentrated in East Anglia and the eastern Midlands. Towns were small and little differentiated from the limited regional areas they served. The Norman Conquest coincided with a boom in economic activity throughout Europe, with England seeing a general increase in population, expansion of urban life, commerce and industry, and a growing concern to develop and exploit the land more effectively. While peasants continued more or less unaffected by the conquest, continuing to cultivate their own holdings and providing service to their lord's demesne as they had for generations, the new aristocracy established themselves upon their newly acquired lands. Some peasant families were able to prosper, though the majority formed a pool of unemployed or underemployed labourers on which the wealthy could draw for seasonal employment. A series of bad harvests and cattle and sheep plagues, combined with frequent and excessive flooding in the early fourteenth century, exacerbated a decline in population and a period of economic instability.

Many towns continued to be founded through this century, though few served as more than regional markets. However, a few towns, especially the port towns of Plymouth, Exeter and Bristol, were developing a flourishing international trade in wool, tin, cloth and lead, which were exchanged for luxuries such as wine, oils, fruits and spices.

England's economy has been marked by periods of recession and growth ever since the Middle Ages, and the effects on the population of towns, villages and cities and the standard of living of the inhabitants of the communities are well recorded through history, as well as in physical evidence still surviving today.

Throughout the centuries the work and trades of the people of the West Country have been diverse and wide ranging, though the geography and terrain of the region ensures some consistent aspects. Information about the most prominent occupations in the region is presented in this chapter, providing an insight into the lives of the people involved in these trades.

## 7.1 Seafaring occupations

The West Country is renowned as a prolific seafaring region of England, with Devon in particular having produced many of the country's most famous sailors: Francis Drake was born near Tavistock and Walter Raleigh in East Budleigh, between Exmouth and Sidmouth. For centuries, all around the coasts of Cornwall, Devon and Somerset small boats have put out to sea, trying to make a living from the often unfriendly waters, with the larger ships more often seen in Plymouth, as the major ferry port in the county, with the Royal Navy also active in Plymouth Sound. The northern coast is rugged with cliffs and jagged rocks thrusting out to sea: a far more inhospitable coastline.

### 7.1.1 Merchants

The seventeenth century saw trade flowing in and out of port towns such as Bristol, Bridgwater, Exeter, Falmouth, Minehead and Plymouth from ports around the Atlantic, including the West Indies, Maryland, Virginia, Boston and New York, as well as from Europe. Tobacco made many ports their fortunes, along with the extremely profitable slave trade. Wealthy merchants in the region lived in large, comfortable houses and often owned large fleets, employing hundreds of seamen and other workmen.

By the end of the seventeenth century Bristol was one of the most active centres of the slave trade in England. The outward journey was made with a cargo of trinkets, beads, hardware, pottery and firearms, which were exchanged for slaves off the west coast of Africa. These slaves were sold on arrival at the plantations, generally in the West Indies, at their market value, and sugar, tobacco and rum were brought back to Bristol. Bristol depended on this traffic and its ancillary trades for its prosperity for over a century. In 1725 alone Bristol ships carried 16,950 slaves to the plantations.

During the eighteenth century Bristol was engaged in the lucrative trade of privateering and it was not by chance that Robert Louis Stevenson in his *Treasure Island* chose Bristol as the port from which his gang of pirates set sail, as Bristol was the haunt of many pirates and privateers. There was only a single sheet of paper between pirates and privateers – the letter of marque, allowing privateers to attack foreign shipping during wartime.

### 7.1.2 Fishermen

The fishing industry has always played an important part in the seafaring traditions of the West Country. At the time of the Domesday Book Brixham was mentioned as a fishing port, and John Leland, in the itinerary of his tour through the county in 1534–43, describes Exmouth: 'On the Est side of Exmouth Haven [is] Exmouth, a Fisschar Tounlet, a little withyn the Haven Mouth.' By the early part of the nineteenth century trawlers from Brixham were important in establishing fishing in the North Sea, and by 1850 the town boasted one of the largest fishing fleets in England.

In F.G. Aflalo's *The Sea-fishing Industry of England and Wales* (1904) Brixham is described as possessing

> the largest indigenous fishing-fleet on the south coast. There are one hundred and fifty, more or less, of the large class of trawlers, smart craft of 30 to 40 tons; there are about half as many of the 'mumble-bees', smaller boats of 15 to 25 tons; and there are twenty or so still smaller hookers ... The number of men and boys employed at Brixham on the boats themselves must amount to close on a thousand. The apprentice, an obsolete institution at many of the larger centres, is still a feature of the industry at both Brixham and Plymouth.

The main catches across the region were pilchards, herring and mackerel. Trawling was the main method used by the Devon fishermen, while seining and driving were more characteristic of the Cornish.

The life of the drifter fisherman was rough and dangerous, but it offered even the miserable seasick ship's boy his chance of becoming a skipper if he worked hard enough, and although work was continuous throughout the season, the trips were short. The trawler fleet stayed at sea in similar discomfort and danger for much longer periods of time. Many disasters befell fishing communities, particularly in the north of the counties. One worthy of note was the 'Great Storm' of 1821, as recalled in the *Exeter Flying Post* of 11 October 1821 (issue 2924):

> Melancholy Catastrophe. About sixty boats, employed in the herring fishery at Clovelly, were, on Thursday evening, by the

suddenness of a gale of wind, obliged to relinquish their nets in the hopes of gaining the shore in safety, but unfortunately more than forty were driven among the rocks. The cries of the drowning, thirty-five in number, most of whom have left large families, produced an effect too heart-rending to be adequately expressed. The distress occasioned to the families of the unhappy sufferers, who looked forward to the fishing for their entire support, but now, alas, bereft of the means of subsistence, is most affecting. The Rev. Mr. Putt and Rev. Mr. Luxmoore, then staying at Clovelly, were particularly instrumental in saving the lives of many who, but for their humane exertions, must have inevitably perished; and at their departure generously left £5 to be distributed among those families who are now become utterly destitute.

Four days later a similar account appeared in the *Sherborne and Yeovil Mercury,* which more accurately stated that thirty-one fishermen had drowned. According to the account from the 1911 church magazine, reprinted in *Down a Cobbled Street: The Story of Clovelly,* eleven of them were from the Clovelly parish.

Despite current restrictions and quotas, the fishing industry of the West Country continues to play an important role in the economy of these maritime counties. Not only does it provide employment for the fishermen, it also generates additional employment on shore, for those working in the handling and processing of catches, and in the support services such as marine engineering and boat repairing.

### 7.1.3 Smugglers

The wild and remote coasts of Devon and Cornwall, the hidden caves and coves of Somerset and the rugged individualism of the inhabitants made the West Country famous for smuggling over a period of nearly a thousand years. Smuggling is mentioned in the *Magna Carta,* which refers to wine 'prisage' and the export of wool. The men who indulged in this illicit trade became known first as 'owlers' and then as 'free-traders'. Preventing the running of contraband out of the country was initially more important than stopping it coming in, though this changed in the eighteenth century.

Most people associated smuggling with the south coast of the peninsula as it was closer to the continent, and hence this coast was more closely watched than the north coast of Cornwall, Devon and

Somerset. At the point where the Bristol Channel becomes the Severn Sea lies the island of Lundy, which has been associated with smuggling since the earliest times. A customs collector at Cardiff, quoted by Graham Smith in his history of the Customs and Excise Service *Something to Declare*, stated that in the eighteenth century 'There never lived a man on the island of Lundy who was not connected with smuggling.'

Given the amount of seafaring traffic around this narrow strip of land, wrecking was also a temptation. False signals were sent to vessels by lighting lanterns, tying them to donkeys' tails and walking them along the cliff top, thus causing helmsmen to steer mistakenly into the treacherous rocky coast; wrecking reputedly sent many a ship and crew to Davy Jones's locker, whereupon local gangs would waste no time in helping themselves to whatever goods were on board.

Smuggling affected the whole of the British Isles, but the West Country's location, isolation and geography of hidden coves made it a real hotbed of activity. Tunnels were dug from the coast to inns and hostelries, many of them given the local moniker of 'The Wink' – the signal given to indicate the availability of smuggled goods. The Treasury, much aggrieved by this aggressively successful contraband trade, set up the National Coast Guard specifically to combat it but was ultimately obliged to lower import tax in the 1800s to have any effect whatsoever.

## 7.1.4 Digging deeper

Until the Merchant Shipping (Fishing Boats) Act of 1883 the records for general merchant seamen include records of fishermen. The Website of the Mariners Mailing List (www.mariners-l.co.uk/UKFishermen.html) is an excellent online source of information detailing how to trace fishermen in British records, referencing all the different classes of record and the availability of documents at the National Archives. The records are beginning to be made available online by Findmypast and Ancestry.

Information about seafarers can be found in a wide range of sources, including censuses, trade directories, wills and parish records, with people working not only as mariners but also in shipbuilding and associated trades, such as sailmakers, ship chandlers, anchor and chain manufacturers, and younger men often appearing in apprenticeship records. Devon Heritage provides transcripts of many trade directories on its website under the directory listings tab and Cornwall FHS has an index to Cornish master-mariners.

County record offices and local studies libraries often have records relating to ship ownership, including registers of ships and fishing boats. Plymouth and West Devon Record Office holds many shipping registers and indexes which can be searched on the online archive catalogue. Other record office holdings are searchable via Access to Archives on the National Archives website. The Devon Heritage Centre and Devon Family History Society are undertaking a joint project to film and index the shipping registers and port books.

Stewart Lenton's *Fishing Boats and Ports of Devon* and *Fishing Boats and Ports of Cornwall* provide a unique contemporary record (2003–2006) of the registered fishing vessels of the region, including fascinating snippets of information about some of the traditions in local fishing communities, together with details of fishing methods and the development of the fishing industry in Devon and Cornwall.

The Bristol Branch of the Historical Association has produced many pamphlets, including C.M. MacInnes's *Bristol and the Slave Trade* and W.E. Minchinton's *The Port of Bristol in the Eighteenth Century*. Many books have been written about smuggling in the West Country, with Antony D. Hippisley Coxe's book on the period 1700–1850 providing an excellent background; it includes case studies and ballads, and has information on places related to the smuggling trade. Local court records often contain trials for smuggling as it was an illegal trade.

### 7.1.5 Hidden treasures

Jack Rattenbury was born in Beer in Devon in 1778. He never saw his father, who was seized by a press gang when Jack's mother was pregnant, and never seen again. At the age of 9 Jack was taken fishing by his uncle, but after losing the boat's rudder his tutor thought it better if he learnt at someone else's expense. So Jack became an apprentice aboard a Brixham trawler for a while and then on a trading coaster. Moving to successively larger vessels, it is not surprising that Jack decided that privateering was the life for him. His memoirs, first published in 1837, covered forty years of smuggling, privateering and fishing, though he is seldom explicit when describing his smuggling activities. These memoirs, entitled *Memoirs of a Smuggler*, are available via Google Books from http://www.smuggling.co.uk/ebooks/rattenbury.html.

The fishing village of Appledore in North Devon is steeped in maritime history; it dates back about a thousand years, to when the Anglo-Saxons fished from its shores. It is still a fishing village but also has all kinds of other boats moored near the Quay. Housed within the village is the North Devon Maritime Museum, which covers all aspects of North Devon's history from the invasion of the Danes in 878 to present-day shipbuilding, including seafaring past and present, with models and photographs of sail, steam and motor ships, the Tudor period of Grenville and the Armada, the Newfoundland fishing trade, smuggling, shipbuilding, rope-making, coopering, wreck and rescue, as well as Second World War activities in North Devon.

The world famous fishing village of Clovelly is also in North Devon. Built into a cleft in a 400ft-high cliff, the cobbled traffic-free high street tumbles its way down past whitewashed cottages festooned with flowers to the tiny, ancient working harbour port. Unusually, the village has been privately owned by the same family since 1738. Their policy is to care for Clovelly and keep it in the style of the mid-nineteenth century, which involves much quality maintenance using traditional materials and craftmanship. Part of the modest entrance fee contributes to this work and plays a vital role in keeping Clovelly so special.

The Smugglers' Britain website explores the amazing story of this trade in eighteenth- and nineteenth-century Britain, detailing some 850 smugglers' haunts and interactive maps to lead you to the coves, caves, tunnels and pubs around Britain's coast.

## 7.2 Agriculture

Agricultural work has dominated the working lives of the vast majority of people in the West Country in the past, and every family historian with ancestors in this area of the country will have come across the term 'farmer' or 'labourer' on birth, marriage or death certificates, in parish registers or on census returns for their forebears. However, the two terms convey different meanings and hide the range of skills and types of work carried out by the holders of the titles. In *The Oxford Companion to Local and Family History,* David Hey explains the word 'farmer', in the modern sense, as 'conveying no idea of acreage farmed or social status; the word began to replace yeoman and husbandman during the eighteenth century … derived from the Latin *firma* meaning a fixed money rent'. The *Oxford English Dictionary* describes a labourer as 'a person doing unskilled, usually manual, work for wages'.

The world of agricultural work has never stood still and the eighteenth and nineteenth centuries saw great innovations in England, with the Duke of Bedford, an aristocratic land-owner in the West Country, initiating advanced farming methods. The fertiliser revolution of the 1850s, when vast quantities of Peruvian guano poured into the country to fertilize crop and plants, saw increased productivity in many marginal areas, and by 1875 farming was in good heart throughout the region. However, a depression then set in which was to continue until the end of the nineteenth century, with the worst phases during the 1880s and 1890s. This depression, coupled with some exceptionally bad harvests (especially in 1879) and the importation of wheat from Canada and meat from Argentina, New Zealand and Australia, meant that many rural communities were in a state of decay by the turn of the century.

Although average weekly wages for farm labourers rose from 8s 11d in 1795 to 9s 3d in 1852, the real terms (i.e. how far the money went) they had declined. It is hardly surprising that by 1850 Britain had the smallest proportion of its population engaged in farming of any country in the world, at 22 per cent. Throughout the Victorian era farm workers earned a very low wage, lived in cramped conditions, and often whole families laboured long days in the fields to maintain their meagre existence.

### 7.2.1 Digging deeper

Jonathan Brown's publication entitled *Tracing Your Rural Ancestors* also provides an in-depth guide to this subject.

Tithe maps and apportionment documents date back to the mid-nineteenth century and list the names of the owners and occupiers of properties. Some enclosure maps are also available for the eighteenth century but they tend to include fewer names.

In recent years family historians have paid increasing attention to the analysis of farmers' business records, including the account books of farms and estates as well as the inventories that list a farmer's crops and stocks. These can be located in county record office archives. Details of tenancies, sales of farms and farm land can be found among estate records, deeds and manorial records, with local authority records often including information about land and property ownership as well as tenancies.

Parish registers, birth, marriage and death certificates and census returns all make reference to addresses where individuals resided, although this is frequently just the village name. Maps and trade directories make it possible to identify likely local employers and the range of occupations within that place. Farmers and land-owners frequently appear in parish rate lists, poll books and electoral rolls, as well as in the land tax assessment lists between 1692 and 1932.

Wills may refer to land-ownership and tenancy, as with John Sillifant of Colebrooke, who in 1761 left 'to Timothy Sillifant my son my messuage and tenement called Wilson in the parish of South Cheriton …

to my son Thomas Sillifant my messuage and tenement called Kersewell in Crediton ... to my sons William and Timothy for life of my daughter Ann Sillifant £5 a year out of my four fields at George Hill in Crediton now in the possession of Peter Tucker and Andrew Matthews'.

Apprentice records, particularly in more rural areas of the West Country, usually detail the trade of the individual to whom the apprentice is bound, and also their address. For example, Elizabeth Lashbrook, aged 10, was apprenticed to Samuel Trible the elder, farmer of Worden in the parish of Luffincott, on 11 September 1822. The location of these records can be found by searching the Access to Archives website, though generally they are located in county record offices.

### 7.2.2 Hidden treasures

The Museum of English Rural Life (MERL) is a major national repository for archives of agriculture and rural life. The strengths of the collection include: records of major agricultural manufacturing firms, historic archives of agricultural organizations and cooperatives, a large collection of personal records and journals of farm workers, company accounts of farms across England and films relating to the countryside and agriculture. The Farmer & Stockbreeder photographic collection alone contains over 100,000 images dating from the late 1920s to 1965, illustrating the transformation of the English countryside from the era of horse power to tractors, and from manual labour to machinery. A wide range of subjects is covered and the collection documents arable and livestock farming, prevailing husbandry practices, the introduction of new technologies and the application of science to agriculture. Many of the MERL archive catalogues have been digitized and are available to view in full from the Access to Archives website.

The Friends of Devon's Archives have many document transcription and indexing projects which benefit researchers enormously in tracking down documents relating to their ancestors. The tithe apportionment indexing project, which began in 1998, makes available the names of owners, lessees and occupiers, along with the names of the holdings and their acreages (in acres, rods and perches), creating a database of this information. The database is searchable by name or by parish and provides an insight into the communities of the 1840s. Luffincott Barton, for example, was owned by Arthur Venner when the tithe map was drawn up in 1842. Arthur occupied a small part of Luffincott Barton (33.0.28 acres), while James Bate occupied the remaining 201 acres and 26 perches of land.

## 7.3 Mining

Three non-ferrous metals mined in Britain – copper, tin and lead – all had widespread and important industrial uses. During the mid-1750s England's lead output was ahead of that of copper and tin. The Romans had for the most part mined the Mendip hills and that area of Somerset remained important until the end of the seventeenth century. By 1854 lead output had been surpassed by that of copper. Tin was not mined outside Cornwall, where it had been a major industry since medieval times; indeed the county dominated production throughout the eighteenth and nineteenth centuries. The mid-nineteenth century saw tin and copper mines appearing just across the border in Devon, with the Devon Great Consols mine being for a time the most important copper mine in the world.

The mid-nineteenth century was a period of investment in the mines of the West Country. Often it was of a speculative kind: mine swindles form the plots in both Trollope's novel *The Three Clerks* (1858) and R.M. Ballantyne's *Deep Down* (1869).

In 1838 a list was made of 160 mines in Cornwall, which gave employment to 27,208 people. They varied in size but five of the mines employed more than a thousand, with the largest, the Consols and United Mines in Gwennap, employing more than 3,000. These employment figures include women and children, as the mining of lead, copper and tin all involved significant surface labour forces in sorting, washing and breaking ores. By 1851 one in every four Cornish men over the age of 20 was employed in the mines, with a total labour force of 30,284 men and 5,922 women. These miners were hard-working and short-lived men, with the bad air and dust impacting enormously on their health.

It should not be forgotten that other parts of Devon, and indeed West Somerset, were also involved in the mining industry in the eighteenth and nineteenth centuries, with mining for coal and mineral paints such as Bideford Black from the early nineteenth century in north Devon.

By the third quarter of the nineteenth century the great days of British metal mining were over, with more easily worked sources discovered overseas. Large numbers of West Country miners, in particular from Cornwall, went overseas to work in the mines of North America, Australia and South Africa, carrying with them the skill and knowledge acquired when a remote part of south-west England had been the most important non-ferrous metal mining area of the world. These Cornish miners were known as Cousin Jacks.

### 7.3.1 Digging deeper

The Cornwall in Focus website (www.cornwallinfocus.co.uk/history/mindbase.php) has a Mining in Cornwall database on its site with over 270 pages detailing the mines of Cornwall with photographs and further information about each one.

On the abandonment of workings, owners of mines were required to deposit plans, drawings and sections with the Secretary of State. In accordance with the 1954 and 1969 Mines and Quarries Acts, and Mines Regulations 1956, all plans, drawings and sections relating to any abandoned mines or seams sent to a district mining inspector or created by a surveyor were required to be preserved by the Secretary of State or by some other person, under special arrangement. In November 1973 an agreement was drawn up by the Secretary of State for Trade and Industry with Cornwall County Council for the transfer of those abandoned mine documents which related to Cornwall.

In 1989 the Health and Safety Executive, the current custodians of the plans, proposed their 'decentralization' to local authorities and, after consultation with the Public Record Office (now the National Archives), the Lord Chancellor's approval was obtained for their deposit in local record offices. Cornwall Record Office now holds 3,500 plans for over 500 individual mines, which include some surface plans, but are mainly underground plans, longitudinal sections and transverse sections (catalogue reference MRO).

Most of the land-owning families were involved in mining enterprises and consequently family and estate archives may include setts, bounds certificates, accounts, plans and correspondence. Records of individual mines or adventurers may be found in the Cornwall Record Office's smaller miscellaneous deposits, while a few collections relate specifically to mining.

Further information on the individuals who worked in the mines can be found in parish registers, where the short lifespan of the men in mining communities is frequently borne out by the ages recorded in the burial registers.

### 7.3.2 Hidden treasures

In 1999 the Cornwall and West Devon Mining Landscape was added to the UK Government's tentative list for submission to the World Heritage list. It was announced on 13 July 2006 that the bid had been successful. The Cornwall and West Devon Mining Landscape World Heritage Site opened in 2012; it is a unique site, covering a technique exported worldwide, including to Mexico and Peru, and consisting of a trail linking mining sites from Land's End in Cornwall, through Porthtowan and St Agnes up the spine of the county to the Tamar Valley, the border with Devon. There, the exporting port of Morwellham has been developed alongside the Devon Great Consols Mine to demonstrate the nature and scale of the operations, with the Eastern Gateway to the World Heritage Site being anchored in Tavistock. This ancient stannary town was the base for Devon's own nineteenth-century Klondike Gold Rush, which brought the then Duke of Bedford an income of at least £2 million, equivalent to around £160 million in today's terms.

There are several oral histories that have been collected by individuals and local archives which include accounts, photographs and stories of mining life. A particularly interesting publication is that of Tom Greeves, *Tin Mines and Miners of Dartmoor: A Photographic Record*, who writes in his introduction, 'this book is neither a history nor a field guide, although both historical and interpretative material will be found within it. It is an attempt to illustrate something of the environment and way of life of the Dartmoor tin miner.' The author's seventy-five plates and text provide a vivid picture of the life and times of the Dartmoor tin miner.

Coroner's certificate, Peter Tavy (1824) – DRO Ref: 1427A/PZ1.

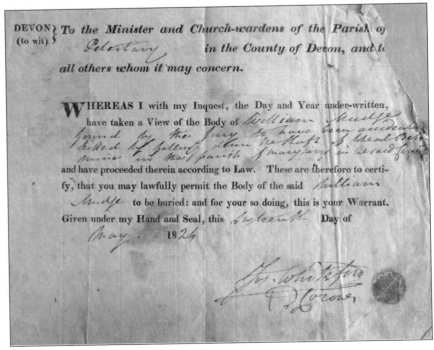

The BBC Nation on Film website (www.bbc.co.uk/nationonfilm/location/south-west) may be searched by location and provides many film clips relating to the mining industry of the West Country.

The Coal Mining History Resource Centre website has lists of mines at various dates, reports from an 1842 Royal Commission on child labour in the mines, and a database of mining deaths and accidents with 164,000 names. Despite the name, the website also contains information about other mining industries, particularly tin. The database is searchable by name, town or colliery, and provides a fascinating insight into the dangerous world of working in the mines, highlighted by entries such as, 'John Friend, age 68, died 12 September 1874. A labourer at the Wheal Friendship colliery, owned by A. Lanyon, at Mary Tavy. John died when crushed by the connecting rod of the water wheel.' Mining accidents are often recorded in local newspapers and further information regarding the individual's family is frequently provided. In rare cases coroner's certificates survive within parish records; one fine example was located in Devon Heritage Centre in the parish of Peter Tavy. In 1824 William Mudge was 'accidentally killed by falling down the shaft at Wheal Betsy mine'.

Lynne Mayers has published a book entitled *Bal Maidens: Women and Girls of the Cornwall and Devon Mines* and also has an online database of over 27,000 Bal Maidens in the region, the word 'Bal' being ancient Cornish for 'mining place'.

## 7.4 Other industries

### 7.4.1 Lace-making

For more than 400 years Honiton in Devon has been a centre for lace-making. Beginning in the sixteenth century, it gradually developed from different types of embroidery, cutwork and drawn thread work. After it was made fashionable by royalty in the sixteenth century, people began to copy the designs and publish books of patterns. Lace-makers then used the patterns to make what became Honiton lace. There has always been a big demand for this beautiful lace. The aristocracy follows royalty so, when King Charles started to wear lace on his clothes, so did his courtiers. By 1676 there were 1,341 men, women and children making lace in the houses in and around Honiton's High Street and thousands more across the towns and villages of East Devon.

The town of Honiton once boasted a huge population of lace-makers, women who would sit outside their houses using the bright light of day to weave their highly intricate patterns. It is an extremely labour-intensive craft, requiring precision, patience and often hundreds of hours of work. Cheaper, machine-made lace eventually caused the craft's demise in Honiton and by 1940 nobody in the town was making lace for a living. However, the craft of lace-making lives on and the skills associated with this ancient tradition are now being passed on to the next generation.

### 7.4.2 Cider production

The Romans discovered how to ferment apple juice to produce a pleasing and refreshing drink. Centuries later the Normans found that the soil in Normandy and Brittany was ideal for growing fruit trees and historians speculate that, when the Normans conquered Britain in the eleventh century, they brought their fruit-growing and cider-making expertise with them. Finding that the soil in Herefordshire and the south-west of England was similar to their own, they started widespread planting of the apple varieties grown successfully at home.

Thus the British cider industry was born and it flourished throughout the south-west of England; every farm had a small number of apple trees, and many local farmers made their own cider via a very basic process, which gave no real control over quality or alcoholic strength. Historically farm labourers in Devon, Cornwall and Somerset, as well as the neighbouring counties of Wiltshire and Dorset, received part of their pay in the form of a substantial daily allowance of cider – a cheap and tax-free alternative to wages. Farmers processed their fruit at a central location. Cider production was a very small aspect of their activity and so it made sense to create small cooperatives.

One such cooperative, established in the village of Norton Fitzwarren in 1805, continued throughout the nineteenth century, making good quality cider to meet the needs not only of the village, but also of the surrounding villages and Taunton itself. It might well have continued for another century had the business not decided that it needed a full-time cider-maker. In 1911 the gardener and part-time cider-maker of Heathfield rectory, Arthur Moore, was offered an extra shilling per week to work at Norton Fitzwarren. With this gentleman's expertise, Norton's ciders became very popular indeed and in 1912 the village business became a limited company: the Taunton Cider Company Ltd.

There are two main traditions in cider production in England: the West Country tradition and the eastern Kent and East Anglia tradition, with the former using a much higher percentage of true cider-apples and thus producing a drink richer in tannins and sharper in flavour. At one end of the scale are the traditional, small farm-produced cider varieties, which are non-carbonated and usually cloudy orange in appearance. These are unfiltered and often called 'scrumpy' (in the local dialect 'scrump' refers to a small or withered apple). The West Country contains many farms that have an abundance of ancient varieties of specialist cider-apples. Production is often on such a small scale that the product is only sold at the point of manufacture or in local pubs and shops. Somerset alone has over twenty-five cider producers, many of them small family businesses.

At the other end of the scale are the mass-produced commercial ciders such as Bulmers (based in Hereford), which is pasteurized and force-carbonated. The colour is golden yellow, with a clear appearance from the filtration. Large producers in the West Country include Thatchers Cider in Sandford, Somerset, as well as Brothers Cider and the Gaymer Cider Company, both of which are based in Shepton Mallet, Somerset.

During the seventeenth and eighteenth centuries a condition known as Devon colic was associated with the consumption of cider. It was a form of lead poisoning, which vanished after a successful early nineteenth-century campaign to remove lead components from cider presses. Lead poisoning was also prevalent in Herefordshire, where lead salts were added to the cider as a sweetener, being much cheaper than sugar.

### 7.4.3 Tourism

Two centuries ago tourism was the preserve of the wealthy. Cornwall, and in particular Bude, was quick to gain recognition as a holiday destination when sea-bathing became popular in the mid-eighteenth century. Transport was an issue, as horse-drawn carriages and omnibuses were too expensive for local people; from eastern England it was easier to get to France than to Cornwall. The spread of the railways in the nineteenth century transformed tourism in the West Country, with two crucial new rail tracks completed: Penzance to Truro in 1852 and Truro to Plymouth in 1859, with the opening of the Royal Albert Bridge spanning the River Tamar at Saltash. Penzance was now linked by rail all the way to London, and the network was extended to include Falmouth in 1863 and St Ives in 1877.

The throngs of tourists were the salvation of Cornwall's economy at a time when the three traditional economic mainstays were crumbling: tin mining, copper mining and the fishing industry. Tourism resulted in Newquay becoming the leading Cornish resort by 1900, converted from a declining pilchard town, with disused fishing boats, into a tourist destination adorned with ladies' bathing tents on the beach. St Ives underwent a similar successful facelift.

By the 1920s many more tourists were arriving by car, heralding the onset of today's issues of traffic congestion on the county's narrow roads. However, today's nature lovers, sun-worshippers and surfers are undeterred by the delays in reaching their destinations.

Tourism is a major industry in all counties of the West Country. In Somerset it is estimated that the industry employed 23,000 people in 2001, with attractions including the coastal towns, part of the Exmoor National Park, the West Somerset Railway (a heritage railway) and the museum of the Fleet Air Arm at RNAS Yeovilton. The town of Glastonbury has mythical associations, including legends of a visit by the young Jesus of Nazareth and Joseph of Arimathea, with links to the Holy Grail, and King Arthur and Camelot, identified by some as Cadbury Castle, an Iron Age hillfort. Glastonbury also gives its name to the annual open-air rock festival held in nearby Pilton. Cheddar Gorge has show caves open to visitors, as well as locally produced cheese, although there is now only one remaining cheese-maker in the village of Cheddar.

### 7.4.4 Digging deeper

Exeter's Royal Albert Memorial Museum's publication by P.M. Inder on Honiton Lace and H.J. Yallop's *The History of the Honiton Lace Industry* provide excellent companion guides to finding out more about the town's famous trade. There are no known historical records for lace-makers and the occupations can only be gleaned from the census documentation and parish records for Honiton and its environs.

There are some very informative websites relating to cider-making in the West Country; one particularly worthy of note is the Legendary Dartmoor website, which gives a great history of Dartmoor Cider, or the 'Devil's Brew'.

Family collections may hold references to cider-making and the Access to Archives website is a useful place to begin searching for further information held at county record offices relating to this industry.

Miscellaneous manuscripts held by county record offices sometimes contain references to the cider-making industry. For example, the Somerset Archive and Record Centre holds a document (reference DD\PH/248) dated c.1600–c.1725: 'a Commonplace book, probably in the hand of Wm. Phelips, containing notes of sermons … building expenses at Preston Plucknett, 1687, notes on horticulture, viticulture and other fruit growing, with specification and rough sketch of a cider will and notes on cider making, etc.'

Bristol Record Office holds weekly accounts of wages and labour on maintenance at Ashton Court between March 1631 and March 1634, 'drawn up by [John] Edwardes and his successors, bailiffs to Thomas Smyth ... Accounts checked and signed by Thomas Smyth at intervals in early part of book. Employees include: masons, wheelwrights, carpenters, glaziers, gardeners, farm labourers, louse catcher ... Work includes: laying new walks in orchard and garden, cutting wood, new gates for gatehouse, building new wall around park, threshing, haymaking, sheep shearing, apple picking, cider and beer making, building and repairs to house.'

Quarter sessions records vary in form over time and from place to place but there may be indictment records recording criminal charges, with the defendant's name, place of abode, alleged offence, the date and place of the crime, and sometimes the names of victims or witnesses. At Cornwall Record Office, recorded in the quarter sessions (QS/1/11/621) held on 13 July 1830: 'Charles Ambrose of Fowey, lab., indicted for stealing a quart of cider, property of Joseph Thomas Austen, esq.: six months' hard labour in Bodmin gaol.'

### 7.4.5 Hidden treasures

In the town famous for lace-making, Allhallows Museum has one of the most comprehensive collections of Honiton Lace in the world. Displays in two galleries feature exquisite examples of sixteenth- to early twentieth-century Honiton lace. Devon Family History Society has two CD facsimiles of books relating to Honiton Lace, Mrs Treadwin's *Antique Point and Honiton Lace* and A. Penderel Moody's *Devon Pillow Lace: its history and how to make it*. The BBC Devon History website has visual-only video footage from 1965 showing an elderly lace-maker from Honiton winding her bobbins using a hand-turned wheel. She can be seen pricking out her pattern using pins 'pricked' onto a square pillow. The film also shows the finished Honiton lace sewn on to a cotton handkerchief.

The Three Bridges Farm of some 370 acres, on the A38 midway between Taunton and Wellington in Somerset, has been farmed by three generations of the Sheppy family, who have weathered the ups and downs of farming and cider-making by embracing change and opportunity. They proudly share their beautiful farm and orchards with visitors to show how and where they make their delicious ciders. The Somerset Distillery is the perfect place to visit to view the age-old tradition of cider-making and to sample some of the brandies distilled in Somerset's only apple distillery.

In the Exmoor Oral History Archives at North Devon Record Office are three fascinating oral histories of Gwen Burnell of Wotton Courtenay, Somerset (born Oaktrow Farm, Wheedon Cross, 1920), Gerald Winzer of Exford, Somerset (born Exford, 1933) and Bill Partridge of East Luccombe, Somerset (born Luccombe Farm, 1916); the many topics discussed include cider-making.

There are so many tourist attractions in the region that it would be impossible to refer to them all in this publication, but this chapter would not be complete without mentioning the Eden Project, a major visitor attraction in Cornwall, which houses the world's largest greenhouse. It is located 3 miles from the town of St Austell, in a reclaimed Kaolinite pit, with plants that have been collected from around the world inside the artificial biomes. The Eden Project has also hosted concerts in these biomes, as well as being used as filming locations for the 2002 James Bond film, *Die Another Day*, starring Pierce Brosnan.

## 7.5 Other occupation resources

Many books have been written over the years about the occupations of yesteryear. In the 1990s Beryl Hurley produced three volumes of *The Book of Trades: Or Library of Useful Arts*, using reproductions taken from the original 1811 edition of *Job descriptions*, giving fascinating descriptions of the many labour-intensive occupations and crafts of the late eighteenth and early nineteenth centuries.

The Devon Heritage website has many trade directories transcribed and available online, from the eighteenth to the twentieth century. The University of Leicester provides a digital library of local and trade directories for England and Wales from 1750 to 1919. Within the digital library you will find high-quality reproductions of comparatively rare books, essential tools for research into local and genealogical history. Searching by location for Somerset, twenty-eight directories are located, ranging from Slater's Directory 1852–1853 to the Post Office Bath Directory for various years, as well as Hunt and Co.'s Directory, Kelly's, Pigot and Co.'s and many more, all outlining the history, geology and description of the county and including information on local government and the police force. There are descriptions and directories for the towns, villages and parishes of Somerset, listing the private residents, trades and professionals within them.

Colin Waters' *Dictionary of Old Trades, Titles and Occupations* is a comprehensive reference book, taking nearly 4,000 names and terms, many of which have fallen into disuse, and explaining the function of each trade from knock-nobbler to wonkey-scooper.

Interest in the working lives of our female ancestors has increased tremendously over recent years and Margaret Ward's book, *Female Occupations: Women's Employment 1850–1950* demonstrates the range and diversity of women's work spanning the last two centuries and suggests ways of finding out more about what often seems to be a 'hidden history'.

# Chapter 8

# PARISH REGISTERS

Church records of baptisms, marriages and burials date from the sixteenth century and are crucial to finding out about our ancestors' past before the introduction of civil records in 1837. Parish records, which are still kept today, first became mandatory in England and Wales in 1538, with an injunction passed in that year requiring every church to keep a book or register to record the date of each baptism, wedding or burial, together with the names of the parties involved in each ceremony.

The parish had to provide and pay for its own register book; they were made of paper, which was cheap, although easily damaged or destroyed. Some parishes could not, or would not, pay for the books and did not purchase them, in many cases, until the seventeenth century.

Several hundred English registers survive from the sixteenth century, including a few complete sets of registers from 1538 to the present day. However, before Rose's Act of 1812 there was no consistency in the way church records in England were kept, and the standard of record-keeping varied enormously. In theory, it should be possible to locate baptism, marriage and burial entries for most ancestors from at least 1600, although there may be gaps in the records due to the Civil War (1643–1660) as well as between 1653 and 1660 when marriages became a civil matter, so many registers for the period did not record them.

Civil Registration was introduced in England and Wales on 1 July 1837. Although certificates of birth, marriage and death provide an excellent resource, the church records completed after 1837 should not be overlooked, as they complement the certificates and hold a wealth of information.

## 8.1 Baptisms
These provide the date of baptism, the name of the child and at least the father's name, although in the sixteenth and seventeenth centuries parents' names were not recorded at all in some cases, thus reducing

Baptism of Margret Sillifant in Frithelstock, Devon, 1677.

research to little more than a guessing game. Towards the end of the seventeenth century mothers' Christian names usually appear in baptism records, and between 1780 and 1812 mothers' maiden names are sometimes noted.

In 1812 Rose's Act introduced printed registers with spaces left for the date of the baptism, the name of the child, the name, residence and occupation of the father, and the Christian name of the mother. This had both positive and negative effects for research; the recording of all this required information is crucial and had sometimes previously been omitted, but the optional extra information which many clergymen had been recording was now left out.

Baptism register for St Andrew Plymouth, 1832.

We are ever grateful to those clergymen who bolstered the treasure trove to be found in the baptism records by recording extra snippets to add to our knowledge of our ancestors. John Hatchard, for example, the vicar of St Andrew, Plymouth, recorded that John James Gordon, son of Edward and Jane Elizabeth Blackmore, MD of Plymouth, was baptised on 25 July 1832 although he was 'said to be born June 26th 1832'.

Some later printed baptism registers saw the inclusion of an extra column to record the birth date of the child as well as the date of the baptism.

Private baptisms occurred when children were too ill to be taken to the church and such register entries may be marked 'P' or 'Priv'. When the child was brought to church for a public ceremony, the register entry may be updated 'rec'd' or 'received into the church'. Sadly, many entries marked with a 'P' are closely followed by an entry in the burial book for the parish. This baptismal 'P' should not be confused with the 'P' used to indicate 'pauper' in burial registers.

## 8.2 Marriages

Until the early 1700s the recording of marriages gave only the names of the couple marrying, and in some cases even less information is recorded, with the wife's name not given at all, simply 'William Smith married his wife'. In the early part of the eighteenth century parish registers often contained a haphazard mixture of baptisms, marriages and burials all in a combined register book, although minor positive additions to the marriage registers occurred in this century as many registers began to contain information about whether the marriage was by banns or licence.

Hardwicke's Marriage Act, which came into force on 25 March 1754 in England and Wales, is often seen as a 'watershed' in the history of Anglican registers. It was entitled 'An Act for the better preventing of Clandestine Marriage', and its main purpose was to tighten up the marriage laws, thus preventing clergymen from performing marriages in places other than the parish church or chapel. Many of these marriages had taken place without banns having being called or a licence obtained, and, except for the Fleet marriages, were seldom recorded.

Following the 1754 Act all marriage ceremonies, regardless of the religious beliefs of the couple, had to be conducted in a parish church or chapel and recorded in a register. Only Quakers and Jews were exempt from this Act, being allowed to marry with their own ceremonies, in their own places of worship and to keep their own records.

Marriage register entry, Mary Tavy, 1826.

From 1754 almost all parishes kept a separate marriage register, mostly using a book of printed forms. An example of the form, from the parish of Mary Tavy on 27 October 1826, shows the marriage of George Godard, widower, to Anne Floyd, widow, by licence.

### 8.2.1 Banns

The reading or 'calling' of banns in church on three Sundays prior to a marriage was a means of preventing bigamous or clandestine marriages. However, the existence of banns is only evidence of an intention to

From the Banns Book for Tetcott, 1872.

marry and it should not be assumed that a marriage took place. The marriage entry should be located to confirm the event.

Banns were recorded either in the same register or in a separate banns book. If the couple were from different parishes, the banns book may record this and also may reveal where the marriage took place, as banns should be read in both parishes.

### 8.2.2 Licences

Marriage licences were preferred by particular sections of the population: the wealthy, widows and widowers, couples where parental permission was needed as one or both parties were under the age of consent, couples where the bride was very obviously pregnant, couples where the groom was in the armed forces, Non-conformists and, after 1753, Roman Catholics.

The licence consisted of two parts: the marriage allegation and the marriage bond. The allegation was a sworn statement by the man or woman that there were no lawful impediments to their marriage, and giving details of the date and place where they planned to marry. The bond was an agreement to pay a sum of money if the couple did not marry. This was usually sworn by the groom and another man, usually the best man, but it could be by a relative of the bride or groom, such as the father. Once the two signed documents were received, the licence was issued to the minister in the place where the ceremony was to be conducted.

### 8.2.3 Settlements

Marriage settlements were used in two cases: by the aristocracy to keep their familial estates intact, and by the middle and upper classes to protect a wife's property. The deeds were signed before the wedding, arranging for future property ownership. Such settlements can provide useful evidence about the marriage and the parents of the spouses.

### 8.3 Burials

Burial registers are frequently neglected by family historians. In early registers (from the sixteenth to the eighteenth century), this is hardly surprising as the record often only provides the date of burial and the name of the person who was buried, without any further detail to help identify the individual. Up to 1812 at best they yield the precise date, deceased's name, abode, occupation and age. If the deceased was under

Burial register for Tetcott, 1825–1826.

21, parents' names may be mentioned, and whether death occurred in infancy. In times of crisis or epidemic, under-recording was inevitable, with the reason for death sometimes being noted in the burial register. Some registers may note the exact place of interment in the church or churchyard, and 'P' was written against the names of people given a pauper's funeral.

Given the remoteness of many West Country parishes, the clerk recording the burial within the register would probably have known the deceased member of the parish and you may be fortunate to find extra information recorded, particularly in small parishes. Tetcott in Devon is a fine example of this, with the 1825–1826 burial page recording Ann Bassett's burial on 7 February 1826 stating 'many years serv[an]t to the late Rector J. Rouse'; further down the same page are listed the burials of Richard Johns Warren, Ann Warren and Maria Harris, all with the word 'measles' next to their names.

## 8.4  Bishops' transcripts

In 1597 English and Welsh parishes began sending annual copies of their parish registers each year to the bishop of the diocese in which the parish was situated, to be kept in the diocesan registry. This practice continued until the mid-nineteenth century but marriages were rarely included after 1837. These copies are usually called bishops' transcripts or BTs and provide a second record, which may survive when parish registers do not. Sometimes, when both still exist, there may be differences between them, particularly before 1837, when transcripts became more precise replicas of the registers. In many cases BTs are more legible and in better condition than the corresponding registers.

Bishops' transcripts are available for almost all Devon and most Cornwall parishes. The earliest transcripts date from 1598, but because they were written on paper very few survive from the early seventeenth century.

No transcripts were written during the Commonwealth period because there were no bishops, and many of the Anglican clergy were deprived of their livings. The keeping of bishops' transcripts recommenced at the Restoration and most parishes have a reasonably good series from 1660; this is especially so for the second half of the eighteenth century.

## 8.5  Digging deeper

*The Phillimore Atlas & Index of Parish Registers* gives details of the location of the deposited original registers of each individual parish, divided by county, as well as providing a map of the pre-1832 parishes and a topographical map from James Bell's *A New and Comprehensive Gazetteer of England and Wales* (1834). Lists of parishes can be found on the relevant county pages of GENUKI, with a search facility to help locate them. Local family history societies (FHS) across the West Country have compiled baptism, marriage and burial indexes, and each individual FHS should be consulted on its holdings, which are generally searchable by surname and/or parish of interest.

Transcripts of parish registers have been made for some parishes and these are generally available at county record offices and/or local studies libraries. They are often a combination of the original register and the bishops' transcripts, so what the transcript says may not be exactly quoted from either source and, of course, transcripts may have errors and omissions. As a finding aid, the transcripts prove very useful, as they are often indexed and enable quicker searching, but you should always try to consult the original to confirm the veracity of an entry.

Many parish registers have been indexed in the International Genealogical Index, searchable on the Familysearch.org website, or on microfilm or fiche at LDS Family History Centres. Findmypast's Parish Records Collection is an on-going project to collate records of baptisms, marriages, burials and related records registered across England and Wales within a single online database. They have published a significant number of Devon records, with 150,000 added in July 2012 alone. Coverage for other counties of the West Country varies, with baptism records for just one parish in Somerset (Kilmington) available to search, compared with over a million baptism entries for Cornwall. The coverage of the database is detailed on the Findmypast Knowledge Base.

Boyd's Marriage Index, compiled by Percival Boyd between 1925 and his death in 1955, is a 534-volume index of marriage registers from many English parish registers by county. The original volumes are held at the Society of Genealogists. The Guildhall Library has a complete microfiche copy and county record offices often have copies of sections relevant to their area. Boyd's does not cover all counties, nor all parishes within each county, but Cornwall parishes in particular are extremely well covered by Boyd's. Further information on parish coverage is listed in the county index section of *The Phillimore Atlas & Index of Parish Registers*.

Marriage licences may be found in family papers, but more often than not they were handed to the officiating minister and are therefore located within the parish records, although few survive. The allegation and bond documents have a greater survival rate and will be found among diocesan records, with some having been indexed and/or published.

Marriage licences of two parties living in different dioceses but the same archdiocese are held either at the Borthwick Library (for York) or the Lambeth Palace Library (for Canterbury). If the two parties lived in two different dioceses, the licences were issued by the Archbishop of Canterbury's Faculty Office. These are indexed by surname on the Origins.net website for 1694–1850 (containing around 670,000 names), along with Faculty Office licences (1701–1850).

The LDS have microfilmed a collection of original and transcribed Devon Marriage Licence Allegations held at the Devon Heritage Centre and a detailed list of the available marriage licences and indexes for the Diocese of Exeter are detailed on the GENUKI website (http://genuki. cs.ncl.ac.uk/DEV/DevonMisc/MarriageLicenses.html).

The bishops of Bath & Wells exercised miscellaneous licensing functions. The chief surviving licensing records held at the Somerset

Heritage Centre are the marriage licences and associated documents from 1574 (Ref: D/D/Cm). Parchment bonds survive from 1574 to 1717 but are unindexed (apart from 1627–30). Paper bonds from 1645 to 1755 have been published and indexed in A.J. Jewer's *Marriage Allegation Bonds of the Bishops of Bath and Wells* (1909). Subsequent paper bonds from 1756 are being indexed by volunteers and at the time of writing the index has reached 1811. Bonds have generally been deposited up to 1899. Bonds issued for 'Peculiar' parishes will be found among the records of those Peculiars (D/D/P) and have also been indexed. Diocesan licence books (D/D/Ol) contain references to the granting of marriage licences from about 1570 and allegations from 1664. Typescript calendars and indexes to these for the years 1583–1676, compiled by Colonel H.R. Phipps, are available. No marriage licences were granted during the Civil War and Commonwealth (1642–1661).

The West Country Genealogy website has transcriptions of marriage registers of various parishes in the county of Somerset, with many dating back to the sixteenth century, as well as providing a link to West Somerset parish register transcriptions of baptisms, marriages and burials for parishes in the west of the county.

The Federation of Family History Societies has produced a CD-ROM containing 18,000,000 names extracted from church and cemetery registers across England and Wales, to form the *National Burial Index*, which you can search by keying in the name of the person you are looking for. The database will tell you which places and periods have been covered so far, since the start and end dates are invariably not 1538–2000, not every county is included, and the records contained on the index are much better for some counties than others. For the West Country the third edition of the index holds 869,000 records for Somerset, 111,000 for Cornwall and 4,000 for Devon. Bristol is included in the count for Gloucestershire, for which there are 181,000 records.

The Devon Heritage website has transcripts within its parish records of pages of burials for many dozens of parishes, after 1837.

Some bishops' transcripts still exist from 1597, though the survival rate varies dramatically. Gibson's publication *Bishops' Transcripts and Marriage Licences, Bonds and Allegations: a guide to their location and indexes* provides a general listing as well as information to help find records of marriage licences, with particular reference to those which have been published or indexed.

The Cornish Studies Library holds copies of the Bishops' Transcripts on microfilm for the majority of parishes in Cornwall, mostly dating from the mid-sixteenth century to approximately 1670–80, from 1737 to

1740 and from 1773 to 1812. The list of these holdings is available at the Library.

Unfortunately, the Bishops' Transcripts were kept in very poor conditions at Wells and because of this many have perished and others are in a bad state. A slip index for about a third of the pre-1813 transcripts has been compiled by Edward Dwelly and is available at the Somerset Heritage Centre and online on the Ancestry website.

## 8.6 Hidden treasures

In a few parishes the marriage registers have not been deposited, or are in such a poor state of repair that they are unfit for production from the strong rooms of the county record offices. The banns book in such cases becomes even more essential to research. For example, the catalogue at Devon Heritage Centre records that Tetcott registers are available from 1596 to 1836. Unfortunately, Tetcott parish did not keep the original registers in a waterproof cabinet and when they were 'deposited' at Devon Heritage Centre some years ago, the boards had been detached from the spine, the volume was covered in mould, the ink had run and the edges of the pages were flaking badly. So the only reference available to marriages is the banns book, which is thankfully in better condition.

Burial registers round off a person's life and many make very sad reading. St John at Hooe, in Plymouth, records the burial in 1898 of 'a male person, name unknown, found drowned on Plymouth Breakwater' and the very next record is 'a male child, found dead on Hooe Beach, about 3 days [old]'.

Online Parish Clerks (or OPCs) are volunteers who collect genealogical information about a specific parish and answer email enquiries without charge. Many OPCs are extremely knowledgeable

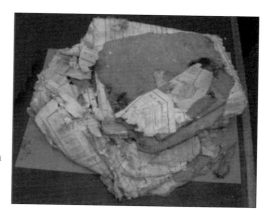

Tetcott marriage register, reproduced with the permission of Devon Heritage Centre http://www.devon.gov.uk/newsletter_may2003.pdf

Burial register, St John at Hooe, Plymouth, 1898.

about their area(s) of interest, holding microfiche copies or transcripts of the baptisms, marriages and burials, and related records which they freely share with other researchers interested in the inhabitants of the parish. The Online Parish Clerk system is very strong in the West Country counties and links to clerks (email addresses and/or websites) can be located through OPC county web pages or via the GENUKI website, at parish level, in the 'genealogy' section. The OPC county web pages often have indexes and/or databases which can be searched online, as does GENUKI; both resources should be thoroughly searched at parish level for hidden gems of information.

*Chapter 9*

# NONCONFORMITY

D uring the Middle Ages England was devoutly Catholic, although some people criticised the way the Church was run, complaining of too much secular involvement. By making himself head of the Church in England and putting the state directly in charge of Church affairs, Henry VIII gave those who were already dissatisfied even greater cause for complaint. Along with Catholic dissenters, a new group was added, influenced by the Protestant movement on the Continent. The Anglican faith was increasingly enforced, particularly after Charles II's restoration, and people who refused to conform to Anglican worship were referred to as 'Nonconformists' and suffered severe restrictions.

The Toleration Act, also referred to as the Act of Toleration, was an act of the Parliament of England dated 24 May 1689. This act allowed freedom of worship to Nonconformists who had taken the oaths of Allegiance and Supremacy and rejected transubstantiation (i.e. Protestants who dissented from the Church of England, such as Baptists and Congregationalists, but not Catholics).

If you cannot locate your ancestors in parish registers, you may suspect nonconformity. However, determining to which denomination they belonged may not be straightforward. Don Steel's *National Index of Parish Registers, volume 2* is a good starting point when researching the development of different denominations.

## 9.1  Before the Toleration Act of 1689

In this period, records relating to nonconformist congregations were generated by restrictive measures from both local civil and church courts and central government, as any form of dissent from the Established Church was seen as a potential threat to the very stability of society. The fear of a Catholic take-over was ever-present following the Reformation, but Protestant dissent proved to be a far greater challenge to the authority of the Church of England.

The first Baptist church was founded in 1611 and a number of forgotten sects, such as the Family of Love and the Seekers (forerunners of the Quakers), were also formed at this time. Most source material for nonconformist history in this period comes from cases in quarter sessions and church courts brought against those who refused to conform to the rites of the Established Church.

Understandably, very few records were kept by nonconformist congregations themselves in this period of repression, but the Civil War and Commonwealth period, which temporarily overthrew episcopal authority in favour of a Presbyterian model, opened the floodgates of radical thought, and the earliest denominational records began to appear after the Act of Uniformity of 1662, when about 2,000 Puritan ministers (a fifth of the English clergy) were ejected from their livings, taking their followers with them. Of all the nonconformist groups emerging from the Civil War period, the Quakers were undoubtedly the most successful.

Nonconformity in the West Country developed largely as an urban phenomenon. The congregations clustered in parishes and market towns with a high population. No fewer than 44 (62 per cent) of the seventy-one market towns in the West Country possessed at least one nonconformist congregation. In contrast, only 94 (16 per cent) of the rural parishes could claim at least one. Presbyterians founded groups equally in market towns and in rural parishes, while Independents and Baptists heavily favoured towns as the centres for their activities.

In Bristol Puritanism found a ready home, and flourished despite persecution. It is said that there were more dissenters in Bristol than in the whole of the West of England and that their meetings were attended by thousands of people. The first independent congregation was founded in 1640, mainly through the efforts of Dorothy Hazzard, the wife of the vicar of St Ewen, their house becoming a recognized meeting-place and a place of lodging for Puritans on their way to New England. Out of this group came Broadmead Baptist Church, which still survives today.

In general, a rough analysis of the pattern of distribution indicates that nonconforming congregations prospered in Bristol, south Devon, south-west Devon, east Cornwall and along the south coast of the West Country in the ports that enjoyed direct contact with the numerous nonconformist sects in London and its environs. In the seventeenth century either conformity or indifference flourished in more remote areas of the West Country, with the lowest proportions of nonconformity pertaining in north Devon and west Cornwall.

## 9.2 After the Toleration Act of 1689

The Glorious Revolution and the adoption of William of Orange as king, jointly with Queen Mary, marked the end not only of Stuart autocracy but also of religious persecution in England. The Toleration Act of 1689 granted nonconformist congregations a measure of legal recognition, and dissenters were able to worship freely in their own meeting houses, provided that they were registered with either civil or diocesan authorities, with the majority of registrations, not surprisingly, made to the courts of quarter sessions.

There were still many legal restrictions on nonconformists, especially Catholics, whose activities were illegal until 1791. After the Jacobite Rebellion all Papists were obliged, by an act of 1715, to register their real estate with the county quarter sessions and many county record offices hold documents relating to papists' estates as well as oaths of allegiance.

The earliest denominational records are registers of births or baptisms. Anglican baptism registers had a legal importance similar to modern birth certificates and the nonconformists, by maintaining their own registers, hoped to achieve equality in this respect. Marriage registers from before the nineteenth century are rare, for between 1754 and 1837 all marriages except those of Jews and Quakers had to be solemnized in the Anglican Church. Similarly, nonconformist burials are generally found in Anglican registers, as the parish burial ground was usually the only one available. Most nonconformist registers were surrendered to the Registrar General for authentication in 1837, although few Catholic and no Jewish congregations did so.

## 9.3 The Methodist revival

The Methodists, like the Puritans before them, began as a revivalist movement within the Established Church, influenced by the evangelical preaching of John Wesley from the 1730s onwards. Methodism gained momentum when John Wesley began open-air preaching, persuading people that they could 'in this life reach a state where the love of God ruled their hearts'. He was among the first to preach for the rights of slaves, and under his guidance Methodists became leaders in many other social justice issues of the day. John and his brother Charles spent much of their lives travelling extensively on horseback, including visiting Cornwall. John visited thirty-two times between 1743 and 1787, including exhausting trips of about six days from London by horseback when frequent stopovers were required. One of these was at Trewint, where the owner of a cottage built an extension to his cottage to provide Wesley and his preachers with a comfortable place for rest and study.

John Wesley, the founder of
Methodism.

After the death of Wesley in 1791, Methodism broke away from the
Church of England and split into several doctrinal groups; in many
cases the divisions persisted until a general union in 1932. Most
branches adopted the tightly organized system of centralized
administration favoured by the Wesleys, and this generated a large
quantity of records. Individual societies were grouped into circuits, and
the circuits into districts, with the majority of records held at local level,
relating to individual circuits and their chapels.

The rapid spread of Methodism was greatly assisted by a profound
sense of horror at the French Revolution and the perceived
consequences of French Republican atheism. By the end of the war with
France the Anglican establishment faced a number of powerful
nonconformist denominations who were no longer content to be merely
'tolerated'. In addition, the inherent conservatism of early Methodism
removed, to a large degree, the long-standing prejudice and fear of
nonconformity as a subversive force. As a result, the Church of England
was obliged to address a number of grievances, such as tithe payments
and restrictions on marriage, heralding the Victorian era of social reform
and allowing nonconformist congregations a hitherto unparalleled
degree of equality.

By the time the 'Census of accommodation and attendance at
worship', popularly known as the Religious Census, was taken on

30 March 1851, there were 142 Independent, 110 Baptist, 12 Unitarian, 8 Quaker, 9 Catholic and 376 Methodist preaching places in Devon alone, together with 8 assemblies of Plymouth Brethren and a single Moravian congregation. At least six denominations or connections of Methodists were represented in Cornwall in varying degrees of strength. The Wesleyans were the original Methodists, from whom the other groups broke away. They were always the strongest denomination in Cornwall and were represented virtually all over the county.

The Bible Christians were founded in 1815 by a Cornishman, William Bryant (or O'Bryan). They were strong in Cornwall, particularly in the rural areas. The Wesleyan Methodist Association was formed by secession from the Wesleyans in the 1830s. More reformers seceded in 1849 and they united in 1857 to form the United Methodist Free Churches. They had circuits throughout Cornwall; most were small, but in the Camelford area the United Methodist Free Churches were stronger than the Wesleyans. The Methodist New Connexion spread to Cornwall in 1834, but was only represented in Truro, Penzance and St Ives. The Primitive Methodists began work in the county in 1825; they were strongest in the industrial areas, and did not establish themselves at all east or north of Liskeard. The Wesleyan Reform Union consisted of 1849 reformers who did not join the United Methodist Free Churches. They had only two Cornish circuits.

Methodism of all kinds had significant influence in Cornwall, and by the middle of the nineteenth century over 60 per cent of churchgoers in the county attended nonconformist services. The Bible Christians, United Methodist Free Churches and Methodist New Connexion joined together in 1907 to form the United Methodists. The Wesleyans, the United Methodists and the Primitive Methodists united in 1932 to form the Methodist Church, which thus brought together all Methodists in Cornwall except the Wesleyan Reform Union. The date at which local circuits amalgamated varied from place to place.

Economic decline, combined with the growth of secularism in the twentieth century, led to a dramatic decline in membership that affected all denominations. Nevertheless, nonconformist traditions and attitudes remain strong in the West Country, particularly in Devon and Cornwall.

## 9.4 Digging deeper

Most congregations kept chapel registers and recorded births, marriages and (after 1691) burials. Some also kept records of minutes of meetings and members of congregations. Many of these registers are likely to be located at the National Archives in classes RG 4–6 and 8. The best resource for nonconformist ministers up to 1689 is A.G. Matthews' *Calamy Revised*.

The BMD Registers website holds records for RG 4–8 and RG 32–36, searchable by name and/or event, with digitized images available for a fee. The indexes are available free on the FamilySearch website. An example of the baptism records of the Bible Christians on the Kilkhampton Circuit (from RG 4/103), is the record for William, 'the son of William Veal of the parish of Clawton, County of Devon, butcher, and of Grace his wife (who was the daughter of Elizabeth and Heard) in the Year of our Lord, One thousand eight hundred and thirty six; and was solemnly Baptised with water, in the Name of the Father, and of the Son, and of the Holy Ghost, on the seventh day of June in the Year of our Lord, One Thousand eight hundred and thirty six at Bethesda Chapel in the parish of and county aforesaid by me, James Brooks Minister.'

Stell's *Nonconformist Chapels and Meeting Houses in South-West England* covers the historic counties of Berkshire, Cornwall, Devon, Dorset, Hampshire, Isles of Scilly, Isle of Wight, Somerset and Wiltshire. The Religious Census of 1851 was a voluntary census of places of worship and a useful list of the churches can be located at the National Archives in class HO 129; this is described, with references to further reading, in the National Archives domestic records leaflet 85. Some churches and chapels were omitted but for each one listed, the census notes the denomination, address, date of foundation and the size of the congregation.

The Historic Chapels Trust (HCT) rescues places of worship in England that are no longer in use. They aim to hand them on to future

Extract from the Register of Births and Baptisms at the Bible Christians on the Kilkhampton Circuit, including other parishes from Devon and Cornwall from 1817 to 1837, RG 4/103.

generations in good condition, as 'the physical record of religious life and a vital strand of our history'. HCT is an independent secular charity and only acquires buildings of outstanding historical or architectural significance. These have included, since 1993, a range of nonconformist chapels and meeting houses as well as Roman Catholic churches. There is no government provision for this as there is for redundant Anglican buildings. Penrose Methodist Chapel in Penrose, St Ervan, Cornwall, and Salem Chapel in East Budleigh, Devon, are two chapels in the West Country which have been restored for community use.

Nationwide surveys to establish the number and strength of nonconformist congregations were carried out in 1715 (Evans' List, updated 1730) and 1773 (Thompson's List); both are held at Dr Williams's Library, the foremost research library on Protestant nonconformity. From 1742 members of the main nonconformist denominations could register their baptisms in the General Register of Births of Children of Protestant Dissenters. These are also held at Dr Williams's Library. Almost 50,000 births were registered there up to 1837, some retrospectively from 1716. The certificates of baptism are available on microfilm at the National Archives in class RG 5.

Aside from locally held material, most denominations have their own libraries and archives centres. There are also many useful guide books published by the Society of Genealogists entitled *My Ancestors were … : How Can I Find Out More About Them?* for various denominations.

### 9.4.1 The City of Bristol

Within a year of his arrival in Bristol, John Wesley took land in the Horsefair and built the first Methodist Church, the New Room, with the first service held in 1739.

There is a list of parish registers on the Bristol City Council website available for download. The list gives the dates of the registers of all the Anglican (Church of England) parishes, nonconformist chapels and Bishops' Transcripts held at Bristol Record Office. The registers contain details of baptisms, marriages and burials.

The BMD Registers website holds several registers of births and baptisms for the Bristol area, including the Bristol Calvinistic Methodist Tabernacle at Penn Street (1775–1837), the Baptist Congregation at Broadmead (1785–1837), and the Moravian Chapel at Upper Maudlin Street (1755–1837) and burials (1756–1837) also for the latter.

### 9.4.2 Somerset

Surviving registers of nonconformist sects up to 1837 were deposited with the Registrar General and are now at the National Archives. Microfilm copies of all those for Somerset are available in the search room and a full list of nonconformist registers held can be found in the Summary List of Anglican Parish and Nonconformist Registers, produced by Somerset Heritage Centre, last updated in 1994. The list is arranged alphabetically by parish and includes details of the denomination, type of register (baptism, marriage or burial), covering dates and whether the register is microfilmed or not. References for these registers are given in the binders labelled 'Nonconformist Registers' in the search room at the Somerset Heritage Centre. Another binder in the search room indexes Quaker marriages, 1600–1837.

It is worth noting that some registers have found their way to the Bath, Bristol and Wiltshire Record Offices, most notably the Bath and North Somerset Methodist Circuit registers. Other church records are

South Petherton
Methodist Church.

held in extraordinary places, for example the Horsington Baptist Church book covering 1814–1901 is held by the Angus Library, Regents Park College, Oxford University.

The National Archives houses many nonconformity records of baptism, birth and burial for Frome in class RG 4, including Rook Lane (Independent), Wesleyan, Primitive Methodist, Zion Chapel (Independent), Badcox Lane Meeting House (Baptist) and Sheppards Barton Meeting House (Baptist), many of which date back to the eighteenth century. These are also available via the BMD Registers website and the LDS Family History Centres, on microfilm.

South Petherton Wesleyan Chapel was founded in 1807 with the circuit covering parishes of Dorset and Somerset. The Somerset Heritage Centre in Taunton has the original registers right up to the twentieth century, although there is a gap from 1838 to 1842. The registers from 1866 to 1906 have been transcribed and are available online via the South Petherton information website.

### 9.4.3 Devon

Records for Devon consist of county quarter sessions order books and session bundles from 1592 onwards, churchwardens' presentments and records of the Bishop of Exeter's consistory court (all held at Devon Heritage Centre). Recusant Rolls in the National Archives in class E 376–377 contain lists of all those refusing to attend regular church services, arranged by county. The North Devon Record Office holds quarter sessions records for north Devon boroughs including Barnstaple 1328–1971, Bideford 1659–1952, Great Torrington 1686–1836 and South Molton 1671–1733.

The Exeter diocesan records also include a number of such licences, 1698–1852, arranged by parish and held by Devon Heritage Centre. In 1852 the responsibility for licensing was transferred to the Registrar General and submissions of returns from 1689 to 1852 were required from both former authorities. These returns, held by the National Archives in class RG 31, can provide evidence of names, description, location, denomination and date of registration.

Copies of the surrendered nonconformist registers for Devon are available on microfilm and most are indexed on the International Genealogical index, available on the FamilySearch.org website or on microfiche or film in local LDS Family History Centres.

Other denominational records may include minute books, which often contain register entries, church membership rolls, collection journals, account books, year books, magazines, etc. The North Devon Record Office holds records for some early nonconformist congregations, generally commencing in the nineteenth century but often including historical accounts and some earlier material.

A box of papers relating to papists' estates, 1717–1776, together with two rolls of papists' oaths of allegiance, under an act of 1791, survive among the records held at Devon Heritage Centre. The quarter sessions records also contain a roll of dissenting ministers' oaths of allegiance, 1780–1825. Replies to bishops' visitation queries, located among the diocesan records, provide a wide-ranging survey of the extent of, and attitudes towards, dissenters in each parish. A transcript of the records for 1821 (covering both Devon and Cornwall) has been published by the Devon & Cornwall Record Society.

A local survey of nonconformity in Devon, carried out in 1794, is preserved at the back of the first minute book of the Exeter Assembly of Dissenting Ministers, held at Devon Heritage Centre. The most significant branch of Methodism in north Devon was the Bible Christian movement, founded in Shebbear in 1815. The North Devon Record Office holds records for a number of north Devon nonconformist congregations. For details, see their List of Collections or the section on nonconformity in the subject card index. Microfilm copies of the surrendered pre-1837 registers for the county of Devon are also available for consultation, together with microfiche copies of many post-1837 nonconformist registers deposited with the county archives service. There are numerous additional sources of information available; for example, local newspapers contain a wealth of useful material, particularly during the nineteenth-century period of chapel building, and the Local Studies Library holds copies of the *North Devon Journal* from 1824 and the *Bideford Gazette* from 1856. The North Devon Record Office holds a large collection of photographs of chapels in the Shebbear Methodist Circuit.

The Plymouth Synagogue was established in around 1750 and Devon Heritage Centre holds records of baptisms, marriages, deaths and burials from the 1820s onwards. In addition, Cornwall Record Office holds some records from the late eighteenth century, including a circumcision register, 1784–1834. There is also the excellent Jewish Communities and Records website which holds digitized images, transcripts, wills, monumental inscriptions and other resources relating to the Jewish community in Devon.

Plymouth and West Devon Record Office also holds a wealth of registers for nonconformist chapels, with a full list available on the

Plymouth City Council website. Devon FHS has a complete set of Methodist Conference Minutes in its library, dating from 1744 and containing presidential addresses and ministers' obituaries, plus many plans and maps for Devon circuits and districts.

Three volumes of *Original Records of Early Nonconformity under Persecution and Indulgence* were published by T. Fisher Unwin between 1911 and 1914. These were transcribed by Professor G. Lyon Turner MA, and portions of these volumes relevant to Devon have been prepared by Jean E. Harris and made available on the GENUKI website on a page entitled 'Early Nonconformity in Devon'. It includes an early name index (1665–1672) to nonconformists within the county and their denomination.

The Revd Samuel Short, dissenting minister of Uffculme, Devon, kept a diary including details of the baptisms, marriages and deaths in the nonconformist population of Uffculme and its vicinity.

The Plymouth parish register indexes on CDs give details of post-1837 baptisms and post-1837 marriages held in the Plymouth and West Devon Record Office. Each disk contains enough information to help you locate any entry held on microfiche or obtain a photocopy of it. You can do your research from home by using the CDs and then obtain a copy of the record if you wish. 'Marriages Volume Two' covers marriages in Church of England churches in West Devon, some nonconformist chapels and the Plymouth Synagogue. Parish register images of baptisms, marriages and burials from the earliest event up to a hundred years ago are available on the Findmypast website.

### 9.4.4 *Cornwall*

Cornwall embraced Methodism like no other county in England. For a community of miners, facing danger at work every day, and farmers and fishermen, threatened with increasing industrialisation, Wesley's simple doctrine of justification through faith and instant salvation offered comfort, security and hope.

The Methodist Conference recognizes Cornwall Record Office as the authorized place of deposit for Cornish circuit and chapel records, and large quantities of material have been deposited, although not every chapel is yet represented. Circuit records may include minutes of quarterly meetings, circuit accounts, circuit plans, registers of baptisms, schedules of property and minutes of local preachers meetings. Chapel (or society) records may include trust and leaders' minutes and accounts, trust deeds, seat rents, membership rolls, pulpit notices, registers of baptisms (rarely burials) and records of Sunday Schools.

There were few Baptist churches in Cornwall but the records of Chacewater (1761–1839), Falmouth (1779–1888), Launceston (1910–1952) and Truro (1789–1962) have been deposited.

Independent and Congregational churches form a significant part of the history of nonconformity in Cornwall. Meetings were held from the 1660s onwards in Penzance, Falmouth, St Ives and Looe, and by the beginning of the nineteenth century there were congregations in several other towns and some rural areas. The Cornwall Congregational Association was formed by 1865 and in 1972 the Congregational and Presbyterian churches joined to form the United Reformed Church, although some Cornish Congregational churches remained outside this union. Records of the Congregational churches in Cornwall include minutes, accounts, registers of baptisms, marriages and burials, deeds and papers ranging in date from the eighteenth to the twentieth century.

The main deposit by the United Reformed Church includes minutes of the Associated Independent Ministers (1802–1879), papers of the Cornwall Congregational Association and Devon and Cornwall Congregational Union, as well as records of many individual churches.

The first itinerant Quaker preachers visited Cornwall in the 1650s and, in spite of fierce opposition and the risk of imprisonment and fines, the Society of Friends flourished in the county, which was divided into five areas, each regulated by a Monthly Meeting. Records have always been carefully compiled and preserved, and all the surviving ancient records of the Society in Cornwall have been deposited at the Cornwall Record Office, by decision of the Monthly Meeting. They include quarterly meeting minutes (from 1668), ministers' and elders' minutes, women friends' minutes, records of sufferings (from 1655), registers of births, marriages and burials, membership lists, accounts, deeds and correspondence, both monthly and for Particular (or Preparative) meetings.

Jewish synagogues were in existence in Falmouth (1740–1892) and Penzance (1807–1906). A photocopy of the Penzance synagogue marriage register (1838–1892) is held by Cornwall Record Office.

## 9.5 Hidden treasures

The New Room in Bristol is the oldest Methodist Chapel in the world and the cradle of the early Methodist movement. It was built and used by John Wesley and the early Methodists as a meeting and preaching place and the centre for helping and educating the needy members of the community. The ground-floor chapel is open to the public; upstairs, the library is located in the Preachers' Rooms. This contains a stock of approximately 4,000 books, pamphlets and bound journals with the emphasis on Methodist history, local studies, biography and critical studies of the Wesleys and their works. There are also major historical journals but no chapel documents or registers. An electronic version of the New Room Library Catalogue is available on the New Room website.

Within the confines of Bristol lie a host of other Methodist sites which carry with them significant aspects of the Methodist story. St James's Church – the oldest in Bristol –served as the parish church of Wesley's Horsefair community, to which in the early days he brought his members for Holy Communion (where the library is located). Charles Wesley's children were baptised and five of his children are buried in St James's churchyard. St Mary Redcliffe's parish church room is the small chapel opened by John Wesley in Guinea Street. Just a short distance from Bristol is Pill, a mini-port on the River Avon from which the first Methodist preachers sailed to the colonies. There is an engraved stone to this effect.

Trewint, near Altarnun, where John Wesley and his preachers stayed during their travels to Cornwall, became the centre of a flourishing Methodist Society, but eventually larger chapels were opened and the rooms in Isbell Cottage fell into disuse. In 1950 Isbell Cottage and the

Affaland Bible Christian Church, built in 1879.

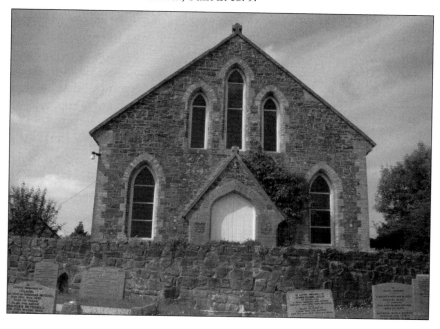

two adjoining rooms were restored and opened to the public as Wesley Cottage, providing a unique visitor experience set in an eighteenth-century cottage and chapel which is thought to be the smallest Methodist preaching place in the world. Visitors to the cottage can hear the story of the first Methodist Preachers visiting Cornwall and calling at Wesley Cottage, see the 'Wesley Room' where John Wesley prayed and slept, with its display of eighteenth-century artefacts, and enjoy a peaceful time of reflection in the tiny chapel.

A diligent search of the buildings of the West Country can often bring just reward, with many nonconformist chapels still in use as places of worship. Other chapels have been converted for alternative use and sadly some have been left to deteriorate. The nonconformists were particularly good at recognizing the date when a chapel was built, and this evidence still remains, often highlighting not only the year of construction but also the denomination. Affaland Bible Christian Church, for example, has now been converted into a residential dwelling with a well-tended churchyard adjoining the building.

*Chapter 10*

# EDUCATION

Before the twentieth century few people saw the value of literacy as there were plenty of jobs that did not require the ability to read or write. Indeed, many of the upper classes resisted plans to educate the lower classes as they feared that teaching them these skills would make them dissatisfied with their lives and thus would lead to social unrest.

## 10.1 Early schools

Some schools were founded in England during the Anglo-Saxon period, and the number of schools in the country slowly increased through medieval times. The Guilds and many private benefactors also established schools, some of them now famous, such as the Mercers' School, a grammar school founded in 1542 by the Mercers' Company of the City of London. Richardson's *The Local Historian's Encyclopaedia* provides a useful list by county of some of the older schools.

By the mid-sixteenth century there were about 300 grammar schools and this number continued to rise. In Devon there were grammar schools at Ashburton, Barnstaple, Chudleigh, Colyton, Crediton, Dartmouth, Great Torrington, Honiton, Okehampton, Ottery St Mary, Plymouth, Tavistock, Tiverton and Totnes. Most places at these early grammar schools were reserved for fee-payers, but some local boys were educated for free. Many of them became known as public schools because they were able to attract pupils from a wide area.

In addition to the grammar schools, other schools were established as charitable foundations either by individuals or by religious organizations. Many had distinctive uniforms, such as blue coats or yellow stockings; indeed, many schools were called Blue Coat Schools. One such example is found in Robert Bovett's publication *Historical Notes on Devon Schools,* where a note on the Totnes Charity or Blue Coat School states that 'as a result of a sermon preached in 1732 on the need for schooling for children of the poorer classes, funds were raised to establish a Charity school ... the school was apparently for boys only and it continued in the same premises ... until it was closed in 1890'. Grey Coat School Plymouth opened in Woolster Street, Plymouth, in 1714, with a small number of children being both educated and clothed free of charge. Boys were taught reading, writing and arithmetic, while girls received instruction in reading, writing, sewing and knitting. The registers of Grey Coat School have been fully indexed from 1735 to 1972 by the Devon Family History Society, though only a name and date of birth index is available from 1914 to 1972 due to the records being closed for a hundred years.

In order to prevent the promulgation of views contrary to its teaching, the church began to regulate schoolteachers, with a canon of 1603 requiring them to be licensed by a bishop. However, from the late seventeenth century nonconformists were permitted to teach, and to establish their own schools, operating on religious principles, to educate their children.

## 10.2 Schools in the nineteenth century

In 1802 a proposal was made for a national education system. However, the government was reluctant to get involved and the Church of England resisted any attempts for the state to provide secular education. In 1814 compulsory apprenticeship by indenture was abolished and by 1831 Sunday Schools in Britain were ministering weekly to 1,250,000 children, approximately 25 per cent of the population. As these schools preceded the first state funding of schools for the common public, they are sometimes seen as a forerunner to the current English school system.

Ragged Schools, which provided free schooling for the very poorest children, were founded from about 1820. The Plymouth Ragged School Association was formed in 1850 with the objective to 'provide Free Schools for the Children of the most destitute of the Labouring Classes'. The Association claimed that 'great numbers of these children grow up in total ignorance of what is right or wrong, and become familiarised with vice and crime, in various shapes, by daily and unavoidable contact.' The Revd Hatchard exclaimed that 'these children could not grow up in ignorance without being pests and terrors to society. Along with such mental and moral destitution as existed in the metropolis and in all large towns, there was to be found filth, intemperance, wretchedness, defective health, mischief, profligacy, profaneness, desecration of the Sabbath-day, and crime in all its forms, followed by the retribution due to society – imprisonment and transportation beyond the seas.' He felt that the cost of transportation, between £150 and £200 per criminal, would be better directed to providing them with an education so that 'they might grow up to be pillars of the social fabric'.

Dame Schools, usually run by a single woman, started in the 1830s, although the standard of teaching varied dramatically. Some provided little more than childminding services so that mothers could work, whereas others provided a basic level of education, mainly in reading and, for girls, sewing.

In August 1833 Parliament awarded annual grants for the construction of schools for poor children. This was the first time the state had become involved with education in England and Wales, whereas the programme of universal education in Scotland began in 1561.

A meeting in Manchester in 1837 led to the creation of the Lancashire Public Schools' Association. The association proposed that non-denominational schools should be funded from local taxes and in 1837 a bill proposing public education was presented to Parliament. In 1839 government grants for the construction and maintenance of schools were transferred to voluntary bodies and became conditional upon a satisfactory inspection. This gave rise to many village voluntary schools in the rural counties of the West Country, with the number of schools increasing by between three and six per year in Devon alone from the 1840s through to the Education Act of 1870.

The Elementary Education Act 1870, commonly known as 'Forster's Education Act', set out the framework for schooling of all children between the ages of 5 and 12 in England and Wales. It was drafted by William Forster, a Liberal MP, and it was introduced on 17 February 1870 after campaigning by the National Education League. The act declared that the ratepayers of each Poor Law Union (in the country districts) or borough could petition the Board of Education to investigate educational provision in their area. This was done by comparing the results of a census of existing school places with the number of children of school age recorded in the census. If there was a substantial shortfall, a School Board would be created.

These boards provided elementary education for children aged from 5 to 12 (inclusive). Board members were elected by the ratepayers under a system of cumulative voting, with the number of members determined by the size of the population of each district. Voters could choose three or more members from a list of candidates, and those with the highest number of votes were chosen for the existing number of seats available. A voter could cast all their votes for one person. This was known as 'plumping' and ensured that religious (and later, political) minorities achieved some representation on the boards. This franchise differed from national elections, allowing female householders both to stand for office and to vote.

The boards financed themselves by a 'precept' (a requisition) added to either the local poor rate or the municipal rate. They were also eligible to apply for capital funding in the form of a government loan. Parents still had to pay fees for their children to attend the schools, even if it was only one penny per week per child, but a family would lose the wage that a child could otherwise earn. The boards could make grants to existing church schools and erect their own board schools or elementary schools.

Boards could, if they deemed it necessary, create a by-law and table it before Parliament to make attendance compulsory, unless a valid reason for absence was provided or the individual had been certified as reaching a certain standard of education. In 1873 40 per cent of the population lived in compulsory attendance districts.

Religious teaching in board schools was restricted to non-denominational instruction or none at all, and parents had the right to withdraw their children from religious education. This applied even in church schools. Rate-supported schools were prohibited from using distinctive religious formularies.

All schools were inspected and individual schools continued to be eligible for an annual government grant calculated on the basis of the inspection ('payment by results').

Between 1870 and 1880 more than 3,500 schools were established or taken over by school boards. Rural boards, run by parishes, had only one or two schools to manage, but industrial town and city boards had many. Rural boards favoured economy and the release of children for agricultural labour. Town boards tended to be more rigorous in their provisions, and by 1890 some had special facilities for gymnastics, art and crafts and domestic science.

There were on-going political clashes between the vested interests of the Church, private schools and the National Education League. In some districts the creation of boards was delayed by local vote. In others, church leaders managed to be voted onto boards and then restricted the building of board schools, or diverted the school rate funds into church schools.

Education was only made compulsory in 1880, since many factory owners feared the removal of children as their source of cheap labour. Acts of 1876 and 1880 prohibited the employment of children under 10 years old, while children up to 13 were subject to exemptions and were required to attend school. With the simple mathematics and English

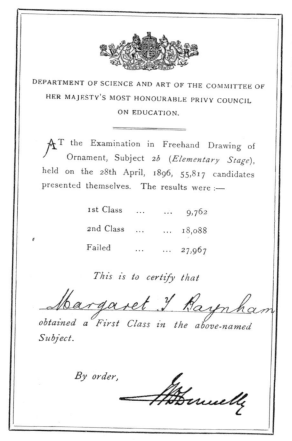

DEPARTMENT OF SCIENCE AND ART OF THE COMMITTEE OF
HER MAJESTY'S MOST HONOURABLE PRIVY COUNCIL
ON EDUCATION.

AT the Examination in Freehand Drawing of Ornament, Subject 2b (*Elementary Stage*), held on the 28th April, 1896, 55,817 candidates presented themselves. The results were :—

|  |  |  |
|---|---|---|
| 1st Class | ... ... | 9,762 |
| 2nd Class | ... ... | 18,088 |
| Failed | ... ... | 27,967 |

*This is to certify that*

*Margaret T Baynham*

*obtained a First Class in the above-named Subject.*

*By order,*

Secondary school certificate for First Class Freehand Drawing of Ornament, Subject 2b, Elementary Stage, obtained by Margaret T. Baynham, 1896.

skills that the children were acquiring, factory owners now had workers who could read and make measurements. However, it was only in 1891 that further government funding made it possible to provide free elementary schooling for all children.

Secondary education remained dominated by public and grammar schools, although these accepted a few poor children by way of scholarships. Pupils attending secondary school were entered for examinations at a basic, elementary or advanced stage in subjects such as Drawing in Light and Shade, Magnetism and Electricity, Model Drawing, Perspective, Freehand Drawing of Ornament and Scripture Knowledge.

## 10.3 Schools in the twentieth century

In 1902 the school boards were replaced by county or town council education authorities which were given the power to provide or fund secondary education as well as elementary education. The number of grant aided secondary schools expanded rapidly as a result. Teacher training was also provided by the government in the late nineteenth century, with apprentices working as pupil teachers for five years in an elementary school and then taking examinations set by government inspectors. By the early twentieth century pupil teachers remained at school until the age of 18 and then went to training college.

The 1944 Education Act was the major change of the century, creating grammar, technical and secondary modern schools. The 11-plus examination was introduced to decide which school each child should attend. The school-leaving age rose to 15 in 1947 and then to 16 in 1974, with comprehensive schools created in the 1970s to avoid divisions in schooling according to a child's academic ability.

## 10.4 Education for girls

Throughout history, the education of girls has been of secondary importance. Men needed to learn as they were expected to earn a living to support their families, but few girls were educated at all until the mid-nineteenth century, unless they were sent to a private school. There were a few such establishments set up in the late eighteenth century, where girls were taught accomplishments designed to help them attract a husband. Along with being taught to read and write, the girls would be taught some history and geography, some French or German, and a musical instrument, generally the pianoforte. It was not until the late nineteenth century that schools with academic ambitions for girls were opened. The number of establishments that welcomed girls increased throughout the twentieth century as it was recognized that women needed to earn a living both before and after marriage, or indeed, in the absence of them marrying.

Admission registers for schools in the West Country highlight the disparity in education between boys and girls. The Holsworthy Chilsworthy register shows the admission of Ellen Gliddon and Albert Gliddon, both children of William Gliddon of Ugworthy Cottage. Ellen was born on 9 December 1866 and Albert was six years her junior (born 9 August 1872), but they both started school in January 1877. Sadly the admission register does not record their academic progress but it does show that Ellen left the school on 12 May 1879 while Albert continued until 18 September 1882.

## 10.5 Digging deeper

Census records include lists of staff, together with their ages and places of birth. Information about schools, particularly special events, may

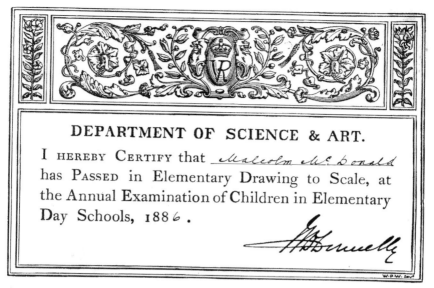

Elementary Day School certificate for Malcolm McDonald, 1886.

have been reported in local newspapers. Reports of school boards and minutes of meetings are held in county record offices or local authority archives. These records sometimes mention the names of children.

School records, such as reports, photographs and leaving certificates, are sometimes found in family documents passed down through the generations, if you are lucky. However, they can also be located in family papers held in county record offices, local studies libraries and other archive facilities.

The name of the school is a crucial starting point in tracking the education of your forebears. You may find the school is still open and in possession of its own admission register and logbooks, or if not, the records may have been deposited at the county record office. Using contemporary directories, it may be possible to work out where your ancestor may have been educated as commercial directories list schools from the mid-nineteenth century, sometimes in the description of the town, city or village, and also in the trade and commercial sections. County record office catalogues are an invaluable starting point when researching your ancestors' schooling, and should be used in conjunction with the Victoria County History website and old town maps to find more detail about the location or history of the school.

Nonconformist schools records may have been deposited with the particular group's archives or historical society, at a county record office or at Dr Williams's Library. Many of the nonconformist schools records have been catalogued and are searchable via the Access to Archives website.

Many public schools' registers have been published and they frequently give the age and date of birth of the pupil as well as their father's name and occupation. It is worth looking at other pupils with the same surname, as many families tended to attend the same school for generations. There are some good collections of printed registers at the Society of Genealogists.

Colin Chapman's *The Growth of British Education and its Records* provides an excellent source of background information, and the administration of the education system is described by Riden's *Record Sources for Local History*. Pamela Horn's *The Victorian and Edwardian Schoolchild* gives an illustrated description of the lives of elementary school children in the nineteenth and twentieth centuries, and a brief illustrated guide to Victorian schools is provided by Trevor May in his Shire publication on the subject.

School archives may contain further information about your ancestors within admission registers, log books and punishment books. Log books contain general information about the school and its teachers, the number of children attending, notes of punishments, children's achievements, health, and important events. The log book was written up every week and sometimes names children, teachers and school inspectors. Reasons why children stayed away from their desks are noted in the log book, with references to 'delicate health', 'sickness of sister' (or other member of the family), 'harvest time' or 'employment'; one particular reference in the Holsworthy Wesleyan School log book mentions a pupil who had a 'liking for wildlife'!

Some log books may be closed for a hundred years and it is worth checking with individual county record offices and archive facilities regarding access to these records.

Some admission registers note the date of the school's establishment, masters and mistresses at the school over the period and an alphabetical list at the front with admission numbers to help locate an individual within the register. Mostly kept after 1870, these registers can contain a wealth of detail, ranging from the birth dates of pupils to their academic achievements, which school they came from and where they were heading after leaving the school. The reasons for leaving are often enlightening, ranging from 'left the village', 'returned to home', 'to Private School' and 'deceased'.

The National Archives domestic records leaflets 65 and 67 describe the classes of records that relate to the foundation of schools and also to the government's role in the provision and administration of education over the last few centuries. The National Archives holds the records of the Ministry of Education and its predecessors, and under the ED 21 series, Public Elementary School Files, further records can be located for various schools across the West Country. This series shows how the character and status of the schools altered over the years as a result not only of the changing needs of the areas which they served, but of the legislative measures that led to the establishment of a comprehensive system of elementary education. The files contain information about amalgamations with other schools, changes in name status (for example from 'Voluntary' to 'Board' School) and movement from one administrative area or county to another, in addition to papers relating to the adequacy of accommodation and measures taken to effect improvements.

The files also contain statistics and information about school premises, trusts, inspection and organization. The 1870 Elementary Education Act made provision for the transfer of voluntary schools to the local school boards; where such a transfer occurred, the relevant papers are on the school file. In some instances they contain endowment papers transferred by the Charity Commission following the transfer of duties under the Board of Education Act 1899. The series also contains preliminary statements for schools opened after 1924.

Class photographs from the nineteenth and twentieth centuries are sometimes located in the school records held at county record offices, and publications about particular villages, towns or cities often contain copies of photographs held by local residents, and many of them make an attempt to name the individuals in the pictures. Websites for specific locations are also beginning to publish images online. GENUKI provides links to known sites of interest.

Property names such as the Old Rectory, the Old Post Office and the Old School House often assist in tracing the history of buildings, although the Old School House may have either been the school itself or the house where the teachers lived. Looking back through censuses, commercial directories, maps and electoral rolls will help to uncover the use of these buildings in the nineteenth and twentieth centuries.

## 10.6 Hidden treasures

The log book of Peter Tavy National School for the start of the new academic year, 6 September 1901, notes a 'fair attendance – a few scholars not yet returned'; on 10 September 1901 it notes, 'school closed this afternoon on account of funeral of (late) an old scholar Wm Maunder who died after very short illness last Friday'. On 3 April 1903 reference is made to the fact that 'the school b[oar]d decided to present prizes to those children who have made over 400 attendances (428 maximum no.) Elsie Maunder 428 Winnie Maunder 428 Ellen Maunder 428 Joyce Collins 428 Norman Rundle 428 Charles Rundle 428'; and on 20 April 1903, 'Reopened School this morning with an Attendance of 15. Quite an epidemic of measles seems to have broken out in the parish.'

The School Register of Admission, Progress and Withdrawal lists on the front page the date the school was established and the masters or mistresses from the commencement of the school. After the 1870 Education Act, a school board was formed for the combined parishes of Clawton, Tetcott and Luffincott, near Holsworthy in Devon. The board leased the former club room built on the west end of the Tetcott Arms from Lady Molesworth, enlarged it and converted it into a school for 140 children. It was established on 10 January 1876, and William C. Richards was the master for thirty-three years.

For Tetcott Council Lana Board School, the records include letters from George Braund, Clerk of the Guardians in Holsworthy, regarding the requirement for school provision in the area, as well as a notice, signed by Joseph Spettigue, Chairman of the Meeting of Ratepayers, of application for a school board.

Inspection reports are also held at the National Archives in series ED 21 and they make fascinating reading. An inspection of the Tetcott Council Lana Board School in 1929 submitted the following observations, among others:

Masters and mistresses of Tetcott Council School, Lana Board, from 1876 to 1930.

| MASTERS or MISTRESSES FROM THE COMMENCEMENT OF THE SCHOOL. | | |
|---|---|---|
| Name. | Took Charge of School. (Date.) | Left. (Date.) |
| William C. Richards. | 10th January 1876 | Oct 1st 1909. |
| Winifred Bailey. | Nov 8th 1909. | Dec 22nd 1910 |
| Jennie McLellen. | January 9th '11. | October 31st 1911. |
| Ethel O. Richards. | November 1st 1911 | November 5th 1915. |
| M. Osmnallack. | November 8th 1915 | |
| Alfred C. Nee | December 10th 1927 | July 31 1927 |
| D.G. Michell | Jan 9. 1928 | Aug 1st 1930: |
| Ruby K. Bastard | Sept 22nd 1930 | |

**NOTICE IS HEREBY GIVEN**

That a Meeting of the Ratepayers of the above-named Parish (or Township), duly convened in pursuance of a requisition of Ratepayers in accordance with the Order of the Education Department dated the 3rd day of October, 1873, was held at *the Barton*

on the *27th* day of *July* , 187 *4*, for the purpose of considering a Resolution that it is expedient that a School Board should be formed for the *united Parishes of Clawton, Tetcott and Luffincott* said, Parish (or Township); and that at such meeting, such Resolution was declared by me, as Chairman of the Meeting, to have been (a) *passed*

Dated this *27th* day of *July* , 187 *4*.

(Signed) *Joseph Spettigue*

Chairman of the said Meeting of Ratepayers.

Application for School Board in the united parishes of Clawton, Tetcott and Luffincott – National Archives ref: ED 21/3858.

The Head Mistress took charge of the school rather more than a year ago and is gaining experience in her first headship. She is interested in her work and the school is making progress. There is evidence of sensible training in arithmetic and improvement in penmanship ... Reading is satisfactory, and drawing shows much promise ... A few of the scholars show up well but many appear to require rousing to more mental alertness ... The infants get a rather poor start in the hands of a young mistress who seems willing to try but will need much guidance.

Across the West Country some school buildings still survive, although many are in a poor state of repair. For example, the Wesleyan School in Lana, Pancrasweek, Devon, was still evident in 2007, in the same building as the chapel at Lana. However, planning permission was being sought for its conversion to dwellings, as well as part demolition of the outbuildings.

Wesleyan School, Lana, Pancrasweek.

Brian Moseley has produced an outstanding website detailing the history of Plymouth's schools and other educational establishments (www.plymouthdata.info/Schools.htm). Similarly, the Bristol Information website has an excellent section on the city's schools with information relating to over 600 establishments (www.bristol information.co.uk/schools), many supported by photographs of the various educational facilities.

# Chapter 11

# THE RICH AND THE POOR

Besides baptisms, marriages and burials, many other records exist that contain information about a parish. Various officials kept accounts of income and expenditure, and vestry meetings were held to discuss parish business. As all records within a parish were kept in the iron-bound parish chest, these records are often referred to as 'parish chest' materials. The survival of these documents varies greatly from parish to parish.

Parishes were administered by the vestry from the fourteenth century until they were suspended in 1834 by the Poor Law Guardians and replaced by parish councils in 1894. Vestry minutes detail the administration and maintenance of the parish schools and almshouses, the church, water supply and the care (or otherwise) of the poor. Membership of the vestry comprised the minister, churchwardens and leading parishioners who were co-opted or elected. In the sixteenth and seventeenth centuries the vestry assumed many of the functions previously served by the manor court, such as ratifying the appointment of churchwardens, overseers (responsible for the poor inhabitants of the parish), 'hedgewardens' or haywards (responsible for trimming hedges), waywardens (responsible for road maintenance) and parish constables (who maintained law and order). Those nominated still had to carry on with their own jobs and trades while serving as local officers.

The vestry minutes for St Michael Penkevil in Cornwall on 27 March 1846 record that,

> At a Vestry held this twenty-seventh day of March, pursuant to notice, being the annual meeting for the transaction of the usual business of the Parish. Resolved that the nomination of the Rev[erend] F. Webber, as Guardian of the Parish for the ensuing year be approved. That Henry Fleming Esq. and Mr James Rouse be reappointed Churchwardens. Mr James Rouse and Mr William Pascoe – Overseers. Mr James Rouse and Mr William

Pascoe – Waywardens. Mr J Rouse, assessor. That a rate of threepence in the pound be made and collected for the uses of the Church and for the performance of divine Service. That a rate of ninepence in the pound be made and collected for the relief of the poor. That a rate of twopence in the pound be made and collected for the repairs of the road. Signed Frederic Webber, Chairman on behalf of the meeting.

Most parishes had about five or six parish constables, although some larger ones had more, especially during the construction of the railways when drunkenness and antisocial behaviour by railway labourers and navvies was a particular problem. The position of parish constable was held in some small towns until the eighteenth or early nineteenth century, but in rural areas of England it lasted well into Queen Victoria's reign, right up until the 1850s.

## 11.1 Parish rates

At the end of the sixteenth century all parishes were ordered to levy a poor rate to fund relief, in whatever form was required, to poor parishioners in their time of need. Provisions of money, food, clothing, firewood and apprenticeships for pauper children were available at the overseers' discretion. The parish rates were raised from the owners of

List of candidates to be appointed as parish constables for the parish of Mary Tavy, Devon, 1852.

property within the parish, which then provided for the parish poor. At the end of each year the overseers set down all their transactions in an account book. By 1690 they also had to include the names of the parishioners being relieved or paying Poor Law rates in the parish.

Those who depended on poor relief included the old, the sick, widows, unmarried mothers, deserted wives and children, unemployed tradesmen and even the gentry when they fell on hard times. Whatever the person's circumstances, the relief provided by the parish would only just have sustained life.

In 1834 the 'disbursements for the year last past and ended at Ladyday 1834' were recorded by James Oxenham and Arthur Venner, overseers for the poor in Luffincott parish. Many parishioners were awarded pay for apprentices, for example, '13 months to A. Venner for keeping S. Pooley, £1.12s.6d', and other disbursements include 9s to Mary Finnemore 'in time of need' and 10d to Mary Ash for 'knitting a pair of stockings for Jno. Crocker'. The rates for the poor for the same period show 'Arthur Venner for the Barton £7, Arthur Venner for Cottage £1.15s, Arthur Venner for Greenslade £1.15s', highlighting Arthur's standing within the community.

Sometimes pauper families were encouraged to emigrate to the colonies, and the overseers either paid for their passage, or contributed to the cost, thus removing the responsibility (and expense) from the parish for maintaining the family.

## 11.2 Settlement and removal records

From 1601 anyone who had lived in a parish for a month was entitled to claim poor relief. This money came out of the pockets of the richer inhabitants of the parish, so newcomers were not generally welcomed with open arms. The Settlement Acts of 1662, 1691 and 1697 empowered two justices of the peace to examine incomers and order the removal of those who were likely to be a 'burden' on the parish. Some parishes insisted on a 'bond to save the parish harmless' from newcomers. Anyone entering the parish was required to pay a sum of money, or have two people act as bondsmen, whose bond would be forfeited if the person ever needed relief within the parish.

An individual was deemed to be settled within a parish if born there to settled parents, or to a settled mother in the case of an illegitimate child. You could also qualify by completing an apprenticeship to a master settled in the parish, paying rates within a parish, owning or renting a property worth £10, serving as a parish officer or, for women, taking their husband's parish of settlement on marriage.

Settlement examination books provide wonderful detail about parish newcomers' places of birth, where they had been apprenticed, worked and/or lived, to whom they were married and their children's names and ages. Incomers were examined by the vestry or Justices of the Peace (JPs), and if they were deemed likely to be in need of upkeep, the settlement examination was usually followed by a removal order, issued by the JPs at the request of the parish. It was then the role of the parish constable to march the offending family to the parish border. If the system worked well, the constable(s) of the next parish would be present to hurry them across to the next boundary and so on, until they were returned to their place of legal settlement.

Ralph Esterbook and his family were examined on 4 December 1740 in the parish of St Austell (CRO Ref. DDP 130/13/3/2), and the settlement examination states:

> Ralph Esterbrook Mary Esterbrook his wife Honor Esterbrook now aged about four years and Benjamin Esterbrook now aged about Twelve Months their son and daughter came to dwell and lately intruded into your said Parish of Saint Austell there to inhabit as Parishioners contrary to the Laws relating to the Settlement of the Poor, and are there like to become Chargeable, if not timely prevented: And whereas upon due Examination and Enquiry made into the Premises, it appears unto us, and we accordingly adjudge, That the said Ralph Esterbrook Mary his wife and Honor and Benjamin their son and daughter are likely to become chargeable unto the said Parish of Saint Austell and that the last legal Place of Settlement of the said Ralph Esterbrook is in the said Parish of Luxullion.

The Churchwardens and Overseers of the Poor of the Parish of Saint Austell duly requested of the parish that 'you, or some of you, do forthwith remove and convey the said Ralph Esterbrook Mary his wife and Honor and Benjamin their son and daughter from your said Parish of Saint Austell to the said Parish of Luxullion, and then deliver to the Churchwardens and Overseers of the Poor there, or some or one of them, together with this our Warrant or Order, or a true Copy hereof.'

The greatest dismay for the overseers was caused when single, pregnant mothers gave birth in their parish, as they were responsible for the upkeep of the child until it reached the age of 7. Justices of the Peace could investigate an illegitimate birth and issue a bastardy bond, through which the putative father was ordered to pay maintenance. These can be found in overseers' records, and the parish vestry minutes may also contain records of proceedings against fathers for the maintenance of illegitimate children. An act of 1744 removed some of these issues by stating that the illegitimate child's parish of settlement was the same as its mother's. North Devon Record Office holds the particularly interesting settlement examination (2989A/PO83) of Sarah Creuse of Winkleigh, 'born in Kings Tenton [sic] – later worked in Highweek, where she had a base child by the master's son – returned to Winkleigh is now pregnant again and putative father is William Pitt of Dawlish.'

By the end of the eighteenth century people were only removed from a parish if they were in need of relief. Following the 1834 Poor Law Act, paupers were removed to the workhouse of the Poor Law Union in which they had settlement. This practice was finally abolished in 1946 after falling into disuse in the mid-nineteenth century.

It was challenging to move around from parish to parish in the seventeenth century, so if someone wanted to leave their parish and avoid being forcibly repatriated, they obtained a certificate from their overseers, stating that their home parish was responsible for their upkeep if they fell on hard times, no matter where they resided. Unsurprisingly, a new parish was much more welcoming to families and individuals holding settlement certificates.

## 11.3 Apprenticeship records and indentures

If your ancestor was in trade, a craftsman or a professional person, he or she would probably have been an apprentice. The 1563 Statute of Apprentices forbade anyone to practise a trade or craft without undergoing a period of apprenticeship. This usually lasted seven or eight years, commencing at the age of 12 or 14, unless sponsored by a parish or charity, when it might begin much earlier, and continuing until 21 or marriage. The terms of apprenticeship contracts were written up in indentures. This kind of apprenticeship was a private arrangement between parents and master, and few records survive.

There are many records for Poor Law apprentices. Pauper children who were supported by the parish were sent out to employers to learn a trade, and thus were no longer a financial burden on the local community. An apprenticeship indenture or entry in a register of parish apprentices normally includes the name of the apprentice, the date of indenture, their age, their parents' names, the name of person to whom they were assigned, their trade and their term of apprenticeship.

Surviving apprenticeship records can help your research significantly as indenture papers required the signature of the master and a parent or guardian.

## 11.4  The last resort

A few parish poor houses, or workhouses, existed in the late seventeenth century as the last resort for paupers, though conditions were often little better than they could expect outside the poor house. The 1834 Poor Law Amendment Act brought parishes together to form Poor Law Unions, each with a Board of Guardians to administer poor relief. Rarely were parishioners now allowed to receive 'outdoor' relief at home. The Poor Law Commission recommended the building of 'a place of hardship, of coarse fare, of degradation and humility ... it should be as repulsive as is consistent with humanity'. A much harsher way of life was enforced for inmates, even for babies, children, the mentally sick, the physically handicapped or the elderly. This new alternative form of 'indoor' relief was designed to save the parish money and also act as a deterrent to the able-bodied, who were required to work, usually without pay, in return for their board and lodging in the workhouse.

Over the years many other functions were passed to the Board of Guardians, including responsibility for sanitation and vaccination within the district and overseeing civil registration. In some places the responsibility was passed to the board for overseeing school attendance and accommodating juvenile offenders. It was not until 1930 that the Boards of Guardians and workhouses were abolished.

## 11.5  The parish church and churchyard

The parish church is often the oldest building in the neighbourhood, and for centuries was the focal point of local life. Looking closely at the exterior of the building and the churchyard will reveal not only its history but also much about the community, its times of feast and famine and the identities of important local families. Rich and poor alike would have been involved in maintaining, enlarging and improving the church over the centuries, thus the parish church is a time capsule of local history.

Churches, churchyards and cemeteries are an important source of information as they contain memorials to our ancestors and relatives. Wealthy people were often buried inside churches, or in vaults, commemorated by memorials such as sculptured effigies, monumental brasses and carved tombs. Other people were buried in the churchyard (and, later, cemeteries) and their resting place was often marked with an inscribed memorial.

In the seventeenth century few memorials were erected; those that were, tended to be made of wood and have not survived. Since the late

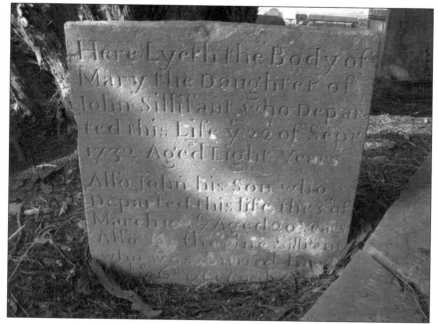

Sacred to the Memory of
JOHN ARSCOTT,
late of Tetcott in this Parish *Esquire*,
who died the 14th. Day of January 1788
Aged 69,
and whose Remains lie near this Place.

What his Character was, need not, here, be recorded.
The deep Impression,
which his extensive Benevolence and Humanity
has left on the Minds of his Friends and Dependants,
will be transmitted, by Tradition,
to late Posterity.

This Stone is placed here, as a small Memorial
of Affection and Gratitude, by his Relation and Successor
Sir WILLIAM MOLESWORTH *Bart*.

Inside Tetcott church: memorial to John Arscott esquire of Tetcott, who died in 1788.

The gravestone of Mary, daughter of John Sillifant (died 1732), John, son of John Sillifant (died 1746/7) and Catherine Sillifant (died 1761), in Colebrooke churchyard in Devon.

seventeenth century stone has generally been used and many of these memorials remain in good condition, so it is not uncommon to find headstones with legible inscriptions dating from the late seventeenth or early eighteenth century. However, many headstones even from the nineteenth and twentieth centuries are now illegible, depending on weathering and the type of stone used. Not all families could afford a monument in memory of those who died.

Monumental inscriptions may note the deceased's occupation or place of origin, or include information about other relatives, perhaps the names of husbands, wives or children. Inscriptions confirm family relationships and corroborate information obtained from other sources. They may reveal the married names of daughters or sisters of ancestors, and may record two or more generations of a family.

The condition of churchyards and cemeteries varies enormously, with some having been carefully tended for centuries and others which have suffered from the effects of the weather, pollution, neglect and vandalism. A churchyard may be overgrown and the gravestones covered in ivy or lichen. The stonework may have crumbled, rendering the inscription illegible. Stones may have been moved, perhaps repositioned around the churchyard wall or piled up in the corner of the churchyard, or removed from the churchyard altogether and broken up.

By the early nineteenth century many parish churchyards were already full, particularly in cities and large towns. Private companies were therefore formed to establish and operate cemeteries; municipal authorities also opened cemeteries, usually on the outskirts of towns or cities, where land was cheap. Legislation between 1852 and 1857 established Burial Boards across the country and public authorities then provided the majority of new cemeteries which were required.

## 11.6 Wills

Even if you think your family was too poor to leave any property, it is always worth searching for a will. Although most of the wills from a few hundred years ago were left by wealthy men, many farmers, carpenters, blacksmiths and other artisans also made them. By the eighteenth and nineteenth centuries soldiers, sailors, clerks and even labourers made wills, and by the twentieth century wills were made by virtually any class and occupational group in society.

In the Middle Ages land was the main form of wealth and by law it was automatically inherited by the deceased's heir, which in most parts of England meant a man's eldest surviving son. A man's property on death usually included personal property such as money, tools and furniture. A man's widow automatically received a third of his personal property and any children would share another third.

Real property, in other words land and buildings, was dealt with in a will but gifts of personal property, called 'bequests', were contained in a document known as a testament. By the sixteenth century these were usually contained in the same document, thus explaining the opening words of so many wills.

Following a statute in 1540 males from the age of 14 and females from the age of 12 were allowed to make wills, though the minimum age today is 18. If a married woman made a will, it was only deemed valid if it was made with her husband's consent, as ownership of her property was transferred on marriage (unless otherwise stated in a marriage settlement) and became part of his estate. This was the case until 1883, and therefore wills for married woman are rare prior to this date.

Locating wills prior to 1858 is a complex process. Before 1858 ecclesiastical courts dealt with probate. An excellent guide to the church courts, the places of their jurisdiction, the location of their records and the existence of indexes is provided by *Probate Jurisdictions: where to look for wills*. Arranged by county, it is easy to determine which courts might have dealt with an ancestor's will.

After the Probate Act of 1857 all applications for probate or administration had to be made to the newly established Court of Probate, with Probate Registries across England and Wales. The Principal Registry in London holds copies of all the wills proved, or administrations granted, in these registries.

## 11.7 Newspapers

Newspapers are an important and underused resource. Accounts of meetings of the Boards of Guardians and debates about the treatment of paupers were common in local newspapers. *The Times* also took a keen interest in Poor Law matters, particularly in the 1830s and 1840s. County record offices and local studies libraries often hold newspapers for their area and many libraries provide access to The Times Digital Archive with digitized images of each article and a comprehensive index. The British Newspaper Archive is a partnership between the British Library and brightsolid online publishing to digitize up to 40 million newspaper pages from the British Library's vast collection over the next ten years.

The award of medals to individuals may also feature in newspaper stories. Victoria Cross winners in particular were lauded by local dignitaries and were likely to appear at many functions in support of the war. On occasion one can imagine the extreme awkwardness many of these men must have felt. The pages of the *Western Times* in September 1916 are full of tributes and plans for receptions for the local labourer and roughneck Theodore Veale, who won the Victoria Cross during the fighting on the Somme. He was the sort of character that the mayor and corporation of Dartmouth would never otherwise have noticed, unless he had appeared before them on a charge of drunkenness or breaking and entry – which the local newspaper reveals he did in 1912.

## 11.8 Digging deeper

Parish chest records such as minutes of vestry meetings, the Poor Law account and rate books, settlement examination books, certificates and removal orders, apprentice indentures and registers are generally held with the parish registers at the county record offices. If you cannot locate them there, they may still be held within the parish. The Access to Archives website is the simplest method of locating parish chest records deposited in archive offices in the West Country.

Some twentieth-century settlement papers may be found in local Poor Law Union records, either as separate examinations and removals or inscribed in the minute books of the Poor Law Guardians. Often settlement and removal orders were appealed, and these appear in quarter sessions records. In the sessions held at Truro in 1842, for example, an appeal was made among others 'by Poughill against order of 7 Jan. for removal of John Inch, wife Wilmott and children Martha (8), Mary (6) and John (2) from Stratton to Poughill: order reversed; Stratton to pay Poughill £3.3s.0d. for their maintenance and also costs'.

Some records relating to apprenticeships may be found within the overseers' records, more particularly in the records relating to parish constables. For example, in 1765, several parishioners in Colebrooke were summoned by warrant, namely 'William Pidsley, Richard Hole, William Sillifant, William Vinnicombe, Charles Tozer, John Brown, Thomas Partridge, John Sobey, John Hill, junior, to appear to show cause why apprentices should not be bound in respect of their estates'. Ancestry and Findmypast have digitized an apprentice register of duties paid for apprentices' indentures from 1710 to 1811, which is searchable by name of master or apprentice. The Cornwall OPC Database has 800 available records searchable by first name and/or surname of master or apprentice, by parish (including nearby parishes if desired) and by year range.

The Poor Law Union records provide a vast array of detail about poor and working class ancestors, especially those who fell on hard times and found themselves in the workhouse through poverty or sickness.

Material relating to day-to-day operations is generally found locally, while documents on relations with Poor Law Commissioners and their successors are located at the National Archives. The MH 12 series contains formal minute books of the Poor Law Commission (1834–1842), recording correspondence dealt with by the commissioners, reports from assistant commissioners and the issue of orders and circulars. 'Rough Minutes' continue after 1842 in series MH 2 and then become registers, recording the issue of orders and circulars, as well as correspondence by name of writer, union, date, and subject, with a précis of the Poor Law commissioner's reply. Correspondence of the Poor Law Unions of Clutton, Axminster and Truro has been exhaustively catalogued by the National Archives and is searchable via the online catalogue. Further information about other holdings including sketches of buildings and registers of Poor Law officials, is provided by the National Archives domestic records leaflet 71.

Many authors have published books about tracing the history of villages and the impact of the church on the local community; recommended reading material is referred to in the references for this chapter. Some outstanding publications are available detailing the history of churches, particularly *English Country Churches* by Richard Briers, which includes All Saints Church, Martock, St Mary the Virgin, North Petherton, and All Saints, Trull, in Somerset, St John the Baptist, Ashton, St Andrew, Cullompton and Holy Cross, Tetcott, in Devon, and St Nonna, Altarnun and St Neot in Cornwall.

Folly Publications Books have books entitled *Old Parish Churches of ...* and there are currently publications on Devon and Cornwall written by Mike Salter.

Groups of volunteers, particularly family history societies (FHS) and the Women's Institute, have made transcripts of surviving headstones in many parish churchyards. The transcripts are located at county record offices, in family history society libraries, in the church itself or at the Society of Genealogists in London. The Society of Genealogists has an enormous collection, with twenty-eight volumes of Cornish monumental inscriptions donated by Cornwall FHS. Some collections have been published and these are listed in Raymond's county volumes of genealogical biographies, such as those for Devon and Cornwall. It is worth consulting the website of the relevant FHS as many have indexes to monumental inscriptions and these can be requested online.

The World Burial Index is intended to record all surviving monumental inscriptions, starting in Norfolk, and make them accessible online. The website is worth checking regularly for new material.

Deceased Online is another useful online resource for burial records, cremation records and grave maps.

There is no exhaustive national list of cemeteries but many of them are listed in the *Family and Local History Handbook*, published by Robert Blatchford, and there are some published lists of burial grounds held by the county record offices. Cemeteries can be found on maps and/or in local telephone directories (if they are still open), usually listed under the local authority. Records of registers of burials are kept, as well as other documents such as grave and plot books. Cremations are also noted in a register. Records of cemetery burials are very important since many gravestones have been removed or destroyed, and some families could not afford a headstone in the first place. These are usually held at county record offices, local authority archives or at the cemetery office, if the cemetery is still in use. Registers detail the name, date of death, date of burial (or cremation) and sometimes the age, occupation and address of the deceased, as well as a grave or plot number which will enable you to find the grave on the cemetery plan.

Examples include the Plymouth, Devonport and Stonehouse Cemetery, known locally as Ford Park Cemetery, with the first burial in 1848. Devon FHS has indexes for burials within the cemetery and these are available by request via their website. There are also alphabetical card images online for Exeter cemeteries on the Exeter City Council website.

Arnos Vale Cemetery in Bristol was established in 1837 with its first burial in 1839. Records of all burials and cremations from 1839 to August 2003 have been maintained and these have been digitally scanned. These and the more recent records can be manually searched upon request.

Cornwall FHS has filmed and transcribed cemetery registers. These are available as part of their subscription site for members.

A brief history of the workhouses in the West Country is provided by Factsheet 29 on the Devon County Council website. Although focused on Devon workhouses and researching in the Westcountry Studies Library, references to Somerset, Cornwall and Dorset are also provided.

Somerset Archive and Record Service also offers detailed information on the holdings at Somerset Heritage Centre with regard to workhouse management and individual paupers, as well as further recommended reading, on their information leaflet.

The *Trewmans Exeter Flying Post* card index held at the Westcountry Studies Library is worth consulting. References under Workhouses for the eighteenth and nineteenth centuries include construction, appointments, meetings and activities.

Most church court records are held in county record offices. Prerogative Court of Canterbury (PCC) wills are at the National Archives and are searchable on their Documents Online website.

Other collections of wills, particularly those contained in family papers and solicitors' records, are deposited in the archives of the West Country and a search of the Access to Archives website will provide a vast array of catalogue references in a variety of archives across the region. It is worth noting, however, that not all county record office holdings have been catalogued and it is advisable to correspond directly with individual offices in the area in which your ancestors lived to find out more about what is available. For example, Cornwall Record Office holds an estimated 80,000 wills, grants of administration and allied documents for the periods 1600–1649 and 1660–1857, as well as seven volumes of contemporary manuscript indexes to wills and administrations arranged by parish, 1570–1649 and 1660–1857.

Wills which were proved in the archdeaconry courts in Totnes and Barnstaple before 1858 were eventually moved from there to the Probate Office in Exeter, as were the wills from the different Exeter courts, which had been stored in various places in the cathedral. In 1908 Edward Fry wrote, 'it was a red-letter day ... when these documents were transferred to their present resting place in Exeter'. Unfortunately in 1942 the Probate Registry was destroyed in the 'Exeter Blitz' during the Second World War, and all the wills were burnt. This means that all the original wills kept in the various church courts and in the Probate Registry in Exeter no longer exist – a great loss for those researching Devon families.

In an endeavour to compile a thorough list of available wills for the county, the Devon Wills Project, in cooperation with the Devon Family History Society, Devon Heritage Centre, GENUKI/Devon and the Plymouth and West Devon Record Office, contains details of over 200,000 wills from 400 sources.

Alphabetical calendars of wills and administrations for the period from 1858 to 1966 are available online on the Ancestry website or on microfiche or film at the Society of Genealogists and other major archives. More information about wills and their whereabouts can be found in *Ancestral Trails* and in the National Archives legal records information guide 46.

## 11.9 Hidden treasures

The Workhouse website has a wealth of information about workhouses, providing details about their location, plans, photos, if the buildings still exist, as well as fascinating insights into life inside the workhouse, the staff, administration records, physical buildings and even memories of those who spent time in the workhouse, including Charlie Chaplin. The creator of the website, Peter Higginbotham, has also published many books, including *Life in a Victorian Workhouse* and *The Workhouse Encyclopedia,* along with regional publications on the subject and there are many references to other published works on his website, including Simon Fowler's compelling book entitled, simply, *Workhouse.*

Many West Country family history societies have transcribed or digitized workhouse, hospital and asylum records, including birth and death booklets, bastardy order books and registers of admissions. For example, the Devon Family History Society has published *Devon Union Workhouses & their records* and *Hospitals & Asylums of Devon & their records* in booklet and PDF form, as well as the *Newton Abbot Bastardy Order book (1844–1860), Cullompton Bastardy Order book (1821–1827)* and other Unions, and *Quarter Sessions Bastardy Returns of Affiliation Orders* from the 1840s and 1850s.

Individual publications such as Tony Philp's *A Social History of Bodmin Union Workhouse* give further information about what life would have been like in the workhouses of the past.

There are three workhouse museums in England at Southwell, Gressenhall and Ripon, each showing a different aspect of the workhouse. Both Southwell and Gressenhall were built before 1834: Gressenhall in 1776 and Southwell in 1824. Gressenhall was initially a 'house of industry', taking in the unemployed men, women and families of the local community. Nowadays, it is the Museum of Norfolk Life, with a range of artefacts and educational opportunities to convey the feel of life for the poor in the nineteenth century and the first half of the twentieth.

Southwell was restored and reopened by the National Trust in 2002 and is the most complete workhouse in existence. The local vicar and social reformer, the Revd John Becher, founded the workhouse, and the building clearly reflects his ideas on how paupers should be treated. Real archive records are used in the workhouse to bring the nineteenth-century inhabitants back to life; visitors can explore the segregated work yards, day rooms, dormitories, masters' quarters and cellars and the recreated working nineteenth-century garden, as well as finding out what food the paupers would have eaten.

Ripon opened in 1854 and now accommodates offices for the local Social Services, with a few of the casual wards open, looking more or less as they would have done a century ago.

Memorials and headstones can offer all kinds of insights into your family history and often provide little gems of information that would perhaps otherwise have been buried along with the deceased. For example, the headstone of Elizabeth Johnson in North Tamerton churchyard in Cornwall reads, 'In ever loving memory of Elizabeth Johnson (born Wood) the dearly beloved wife of Owen Johnson of Zululand, South Africa, who fell asleep Oct. 10th 1929 whilst on holiday aged 60 years'.

In Northam in the north of Devon Serafino P. Turcich is remembered with a headstone marking his grave: 'Sacred in the memory of Serafino P. Turcich of Fuime, mate of the Austrian Barque Pace wrecked on the Northam Sands Dec 28 1868 Aged 21'. Three other crew members are also remembered on his grave, though not named: 'three of the Crew of the same ship interred adjoining this Grave'.

Inside the church in Colebrooke, Devon, is an extremely large memorial plaque detailing several generations of the wealthy Sillifant family, who owned Coombe House, the local manor house in the village. However, the memorial makes sad reading, with one family losing seven of their eight children. John, the last surviving son of John and Mary Ann Sillifant, is remembered, along with his wife Caroline and their four children.

Sometimes wills after 1858 are little more than two pages with limited information, in addition to what is on the alphabetical annual index. Purchasing a will from the Probate Registry carries a standard charge no matter the length of the will. Wills can run to many dozens of pages and provide information about the extended family as well as other members of the community and extensive financial detail regarding the deceased's estate. Francis Synge Sillifant's will is one such document; totalling thirty-four pages, it is scarcely possible that Francis missed any member of his family out of his last will and testament!

Part of the memorial plaque inside Colebrooke Church, Devon.

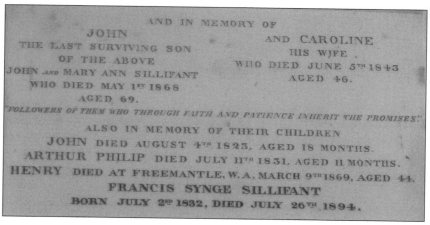

BE IT KNOWN that at the date hereunder written the last Will and

Testament *as contained in Writings marked A B and C*

of *Francis Synge Sillifant of N° 17 Beacon,*

*Exmouth, formerly of Wear Gifford, both in the*

*County of Devon, Esquire* —————————————

deceased, who died on the *26th* day of *July* ——— 18*94*

at *N° 22 East Southernhay in the County of the*

*City of Exeter* and who at the time of *his* death had a fixed place of abode

at *Exmouth* ————————————— within the District

of *the County of Devon* —————— —— —

was proved and registered in the District Probate Registry of Her Majesty's High

Court of Justice at *Exeter* ——————— and that Adminis-

tration of the personal estate of the said deceased was granted by the aforesaid Court

to *The Reverend Charles William Sillifant*

*of Hooll, in the County of Dorset, Clerk, Brother*

*of the deceased and Vincent Waldo Calmady*

*Hamlyn of Leawood House, Bridestowe, in*

*the County of Devon, Esquire, two of the*

*Executors* —————————————————

named in the said *Will, they* ——— having been first sworn well

and faithfully to administer the same. *Power being reserved*

*of making the like Grant to Fanny*

*Gertrude Sillifant, Widow, the Relict of*

*the deceased, the other Executor.*

Dated the *19th* day of *December* — 18*94*

Gross value of Personal Estate £ *14,680 . 0 . 8*

Net value  „  „  £ *14,422 . 11 . 5*

Extracted by *Ford Harris & Ford,*
*Solicitors, Exeter*

205

W B & L (075w)—44890—40000—4/64

The first page of the 1894 will of Francis Synge Sillifant.

# Chapter 12

# MIGRATION

Throughout history people have emigrated for many reasons – to escape religious persecution, transportation for crimes committed, service in the armed forces or for business reasons – and then settled abroad. However, most emigrants leave for economic reasons, especially poverty at home and the prospect of a new and better life abroad.

## 12.1 Seventeenth century

During the early seventeenth century there was a great deal of religious persecution in England resulting in the birth of two main movements, the Puritans and the Separatists, both of which sought greater freedom of worship. From as early as 1607 the religious congregations of Brownist English Dissenters fled the volatile political environment in the East Midlands of England for the relative calm and tolerance of Holland. Concerned with losing their cultural identity, the group later arranged with English investors to establish a new colony in North America. A new phase began when the *Mayflower* carrying the Pilgrim Fathers landed a group of separatists at Cape Cod on Christmas Day in 1620. The colony became the second successful English settlement, after the founding of Jamestown, Virginia, in 1607, and later the oldest continuously inhabited British settlement in what was to become the United States of America. The Pilgrims' story of seeking religious freedom has become a central theme of the history and culture of the United States.

In Dorchester, Dorset, a Puritan Minister, the Reverend John White (1575–1648), the rector of both Holy Trinity and St Peter's, was inspired by this new adventure and saw the potential for a Puritan settlement as well. He started raising capital, enlisting the support of influential people, and recruiting followers to move to New England. In 1622 they formed the 'Dorchester Company' to take forward the enterprise. Although this initial effort failed, White refused to abandon his plans and a new company, the 'New England Company', bought the debts and assets of the old company, commissioning two ships in 1627/8 to sail with supplies from Weymouth to New England.

As there were no passenger lists it is difficult to know which pilgrims arrived on which ship, but the two ships successfully sailed to New England in 1628/9. Another followed in 1630, when White organised a major emigration of 140 people from Somerset, Dorset and Devon, specifically from the towns of Dorchester, Bridport, Crewkerne and Exeter. They set sail from Plymouth on 20 March 1630 on board the *Mary & John*, and arrived at Nantasket Point, now called Dorchester, in Massachusetts.

From about 1617 until the outbreak of the American War of Independence in 1775, the law courts of England and Wales, and also Scotland, provided another major group of emigrants to America. Many of the men, women and children who fell foul of the law received a sentence of transportation, usually for seven to fourteen years. A number were vagrants, while others were criminals (either serious or petty), rebels or even prisoners of war.

Some inhabitants of the West Country travelled to the colonies as indentured servants. The American farmers, planters and shopkeepers found it difficult to hire free workers, primarily because it was so easy for potential workers to set up their own farms. So they would pay the passage of a young worker from England who would work for several years to pay off the travel costs debt. During the indenture period the servants were not paid wages, but were provided with food, accommodation, clothing and training.

## 12.2 Eighteenth century

It was not until the late eighteenth century that new destinations for emigration presented themselves in Australia, New Zealand and Canada. The transportation of convicts to America continued until 1776, and to Australia from 1788 to 1868, with some also being sent to South Africa during this period.

Free settlers also sailed to Australia in search of land and work; they formed small communities and built their own homes. For them it was a country of hope and promise. For convicts, however, the immediate prospect was not dissimilar to slave labour. The weakest did not survive the voyage: 26 per cent of those on the second fleet died at sea, and another 14 per cent died within eight months of landing.

The first Britons ventured to New Zealand in about 1790 but there was little emigration before 1840 when the country became a crown colony.

The British settlement of Canada began in the mid-seventeenth century, with small outposts of the Hudson Bay Company, and by 1763 Britain controlled the whole of eastern Canada. The population remained relatively small but was boosted in 1776 by 70,000 or so Loyalists fleeing from the newly independent United States of America.

## 12.3 Nineteenth century

Emigration from England in the nineteenth century was centred on the major ports of Liverpool and London, but for migrants from the West Country either would have necessitated a very long journey, especially before the railways. Ports on the north and south coasts of Devon and Cornwall were therefore important ports of departure for early migrants, in particular Padstow, Appledore, Dartmouth, Exeter, Teignmouth, Bideford, St Ives, Falmouth and Plymouth. Nowhere in the West Country was far from the coast; for most, the coast was within a day's horse journey.

During the long period of the Napoleonic Wars the farmers in the West Country were prosperous. There was no competition from imported grain, so prices were high. In turn, rent and rates could be paid, poor land brought into cultivation and work provided for many. With the coming of peace in 1815 and the return of normal international trade, grain was imported once more and it was not long before prices fell and farmers could not afford to employ as many people as before. Coupled with the soldiers' return home, this caused high levels of unemployment, particularly in the rural areas of the region. The extreme poverty and its consequences, which stemmed initially from the agricultural depression, left many families with no alternative but to look elsewhere for a means of survival.

Farming was widespread in all parts of Cornwall, Devon and Somerset but the parishes where agriculture was predominant were in the north-east corner of Cornwall, the north of Devon, the west of Somerset and in the coastal areas generally. The first phase of the emigration of members of the farming community started soon after 1815, reached a peak in 1822–1823 and continued until the 1830s. In the next decade came the 'Hungry Forties', which led to another wave of emigration of agricultural workers. This was repeated during the farming depression which started in the mid-1870s and lasted for nearly twenty years.

During the times when the agricultural industry did not prosper, some farm workers who lived in the mining areas were able to obtain work in the mines but the numbers of unemployed that could be absorbed were limited. Mining fortunes rose and fell and many who started on the land may have emigrated later as miners.

For hundreds of years tin and copper ores were extracted in Devon and Cornwall and refined in South Wales. Ships plied the ore up the Bristol Channel, with 10,000 tons per year being transported, involving 150 ships at the end of the eighteenth century. The north coast docks were therefore ready for the masted schooners and clippers used to carry emigrants. Miners in Devon and Cornwall left the counties when the mines ceased to be worked or when better opportunities presented themselves, either abroad or in other areas of England and Wales. Depending on the price of tin and copper, the fortunes of the inhabitants of the mining districts rose and fell. It was not until the 1870s that the final decline set in, which was accompanied by a mass exodus of miners from the West Country. Mining, at least for the working miner, had always been hard and hazardous, with just enough reward to keep a family above the poverty level, if the ground was productive and the quality of ore was high. Even when a miner was in work, there was little to lose in deciding to emigrate to another country where minerals were being discovered. If a mine closed down, with no hope of alternative employment, emigration was an attractive option.

At first, there was little or no governmental involvement with emigration. The would-be emigrant had to make his own way abroad once he had a few pounds saved or borrowed. At this time a cheap passage – albeit a very uncomfortable one – could be obtained from Padstow and Bideford to Canada and the United States of America on vessels that had offloaded their cargoes of timber to these ports.

By the 1830s the transatlantic passenger trade was developing and local newspapers carried regular advertisements for vessels about to sail for Canada or America from ports in Devon and Cornwall, particularly Falmouth and Plymouth. Many smaller ports provided transport to the main centres of embarkation. During the 1830s vessels charged £3 a head (children at reduced rates), but comfort and amenities were minimal. By the end of the 1830s emigration agents appointed by the Colonization Commission were to be found in most towns in the region. They were able to give advice to prospective settlers about the situation and terms of tenure of available crown land in Canada, Australia and New Zealand. They also administered the 'Assisted Passage' schemes, introduced to help those unable to afford their passage, but who were considered likely to become good colonists.

The Poor Law Act of 1834 permitted Poor Law Unions to supply money, clothing or goods to poor families for their passage to the colonies; this assistance continued until 1890. From 1836 to 1846 Boards of Guardians assisted about 14,000 English and Welsh people to emigrate, particularly to Canada. The Workhouse website is an excellent resource for further reading on this subject, as is an article by Graham Davis entitled 'Shovelling out paupers?: Emigration from Ireland and the South-West of England, 1815–1850', made available in PDF via the Bath Spa University website.

Many instances of the assistance provided by the Boards of Guardians can be located in the National Archives in section MH 12. For example, in 1843 Charles Bond, the clerk to the Guardians of the Axminster Poor Law Union, wrote a note regarding emigration to Canada. He refers to a letter received from the Commission on 12 August, which was under consideration by the Board of Guardians:

> They are requesting approval of the grant made to Jane Jeffrey, age 33, a widow of Hawkchurch. They were unwilling to delay matters further as 'the season is far advanced for such a voyage' – the money will cover the passage and allow for purchase of some clothing. Jeffrey has friends in Canada who are anxious for her to join them. She has six children: Silvanus Jeffrey (14), Elizabeth Jeffrey (11), Matilda Jeffrey (9), Edward Jeffrey (7), John Jeffrey (5), and Thomas Jeffrey (3).' (Paper Number: 10793/A/1843. *See also* Paper Number: 9419/A/1843. Poor Law Union Number 76. Counties: Devon and Dorset. Date 6 September 1843. Catalogue reference MH 12/2097/97.)

In 1844 'Charles Bond ... forwards the resolution of the Hawkchurch parish meeting regarding the emigration of Jane Jeffrey and her six children. The guardians request permission to provide £30 for the family.' (Paper Number: 4068/A/1844. Poor Law Union Number 76. Counties: Devon and Dorset. Date 4 April 1844. Catalogue reference MH 12/2097/173 Folios 291–293.)

Assistance was also provided by the Colonial Land and Emigration Office, which was established in 1833 to aid emigration by making land grants and providing free passage. By 1869 it had assisted about 300,000 British and Irish people to emigrate.

The first wave of emigration followed the victory at Waterloo in 1815, and the third wave was brought about by the 1870s farming depression. During this sixty-year period the colonies and America had developed greatly both economically and socially, and travel to distant shores was less of an ordeal. The introduction of larger ships on the transatlantic run necessitated a journey to Liverpool or Southampton, but with the spreading network of railways, this was less difficult.

Often married miners left their families at home, sending remittances from time to time. If the new country offered a better future, the family joined the emigrant, but if things didn't work out, the family might never hear from their 'breadwinner' again.

In the second half of the nineteenth century many organizations arranged the emigration of poor children or orphans to Australia, Canada, New Zealand or other parts of the Empire, to start a new life. The Poor Law Amendment Act of 1850 allowed Boards of Guardians to send children under the age of 16 overseas. Between 1869 and 1948 at least 100,000 children were sent from Britain to new homes in Canada and about 50,000 were sent to Australia, New Zealand and South Africa, including a few thousand after the Second World War.

The Library and Archives Canada website provides a searchable database of Home Children (1869–1930). Many orphan emigrations of West Country children are noted, including Leslie C. Hutt, taken into care in Bristol and sent to Canada in 1909 aged 12 by an agent, Mrs Birt, to undertake active service. Other agents referred to within the database include the Salvation Army, Dr Barnardo's and the Catholic Emigration Society.

## 12.4 Digging deeper

Sadly, neither county record offices nor the National Archives hold comprehensive lists of emigrants. Lists of emigrants on particular ships were compiled at the port of disembarkation. Even today, there is no compulsory record of the emigration of individuals. Records of emigrants held at the National Archives are detailed in the National Archives domestic records leaflet 107, with the main sources being contained in the records of the Colonial Office, the Board of Trade, the Treasury and the Home Office.

Findmypast has outgoing passenger lists indexed from 1890 to 1960, and Ancestry has incoming passenger lists indexed from 1878 to 1960.

Passenger lists for destinations outside Europe are generally only available from 1890 to 1960. These are in the National Archives series BT 27, listing passenger name, occupation, age and destination. The lists are arranged by year, by port, and then in chronological order of the date of sailing, so the vessel's name and the date of travel are required in order to start searching.

A few pre-1890 passenger lists have survived and are held at the National Archives. There are several websites which provide transcripts of passenger lists and correspondence, the Ships List and Emigrants websites being particularly worthy of note.

County record offices may hold some evidence relating to the transportation of convicts, with many cases found in the papers of the county quarter sessions, as well as other crime-related records such as transportation bonds and contracts.

The GENUKI website provides many references, links to websites and other useful material under the 'emigration and immigration' section for particular West Country counties, or indeed for individual cities, towns and villages, with some superb articles on the subject made available online by volunteers.

## 12.5  Hidden treasures

In 1654 Bristol City Council passed an ordinance requiring that a register of servants destined for the colonies be kept, to prevent the practice of dumping innocent youths into servitude. The registers, covering the period 1654 to 1686, are the largest body of indenture records known, and they are also a unique record of English emigration to the American colonies. Of the total of 10,000 servants in these registers, almost all came from the West Country, the West Midlands or Wales. Most entries give the name of the servant, his place of origin (until 1661), length of service, destination (usually Virginia, Maryland or the West Indies), name of master, and, after 1670, the name of the ship. These have been made available on the Ancestry website with four indexes included, one each for servants, masters, places of origin and ships.

## 12.6  Emigration to Australia

Australia was discovered by Captain Cook in 1770, and a penal colony was established by the First Fleet which arrived in January 1788, in what became New South Wales. A second fleet followed in 1790 and a third in 1791; it is estimated that between 1788 and 1868 about 162,000 men and women were transported from Britain to Australia. Australia also attracted free settlers such as traders and farmers whose numbers soared after the discovery of gold in the 1850s.

From 1832 the British government gave assistance to those wishing to emigrate, and many of the inhabitants of the rural areas of the West Country took advantage of these 'Assisted Emigration Schemes' once the potential for agriculture and sheep farming was realized.

### 12.6.1  Digging deeper

All eight ex-colonies are separate states and territories with their own archives. The Commonwealth of Australia, formed in 1901, has a federal archive in the capital, Canberra, and records of grants of land are held in the individual states.

The 1828 census for New South Wales is held at the National Archives in series HO 10, and details over 35,000 people. Passenger lists are obviously a great help and these are discussed in section 12.4 above, with passenger lists from before 1890 noted in Andrew Peake's *National Register of Shipping Arrivals, Australia and New Zealand*. Many other key records are held at the National Archives of Australia and their catalogue is simple to search.

The State Library of Queensland website has a very thorough reference guide to locating immigration records in Australia's various states.

Trial records may briefly mention a transported ancestor's background and conviction, although better sources of information are clemency petitions held in the National Archives in series HO 17 and HO 18, with an index in HO 19. Convicts, once they had served their sentence, sometimes petitioned for their families to be granted free passage to Australia to reunite the family. Petitions and accompanying papers containing family details are located in series PC 1 and HO 12.

Migration documentation can be located on the National Archives of Australia website, which is searchable by name. Many documents have been digitized and copies are available online.

The National Library of Australia's subject guides and documents are an excellent source of information, for example, 'The Somerset years: government-assisted emigrants from Somerset and Bristol who arrived in Port Phillip/Victoria 1839–1854'. Other migration records are searchable through *Trove*, which catalogues 305,635,385 Australian online resources, including books, images, historic newspapers, maps, music and archives.

### 12.6.2 *Hidden treasures*

The Cornwall Online Parish Clerks have listed numerous resources, links, databases and other items to search for Cornish ancestors in Australia, to help bring the past alive and track down your forebears who travelled down under (http://cornwall-opc.org/Structure/resources.php). The Ancestry website has made available many Australian convict records, including the Convict Index 1788–1868 and various New South Wales resources, such as the Colonial Secretary's Papers 1788–1825, Convict Indents 1788–1842, Gaol Description and Entrance Books 1818–1930, Tickets of Leave, 1824–1867 and Convict

Registers of Conditional and Absolute Pardons 1791–1867. Used together, these resources can provide a documented history of the life of a transported convict.

At the Summer Assizes in Devon on 11 August 1821, for example, John Maunder was found guilty of 'larceny of the person'. He was sentenced to transportation for life. Transported on the Asia 2 and then the *Phoenix*, John arrived in Australia in 1822. He was tried in New South Wales according to the Colonial Secretary's Papers, but was found

Ticket of leave for John Maunder, granted 1 October 1833. (State Archives NSW; Series: NRS 12202; Item: [4/4090]; Reel: 920.)

not guilty of burglary on 24 February 1825. His ticket of leave was granted on 1 October 1833 and he received a conditional pardon on 28 October 1840.

As well as holding convict records for Australia, Ancestry has the New South Wales Unassisted Passenger Lists from 1826 to 1922, containing details of the ship, passengers' names and occupations, ports of departure, arrival dates and possibly bills of health. For those individuals whose journeys were subsidized or paid for by another person or agency, the records of Assisted Immigrants entering New South Wales for 1828–1896 are also available. The database holds three different types of record: returns of convicts' applications for wives and families, persons on bounty ships (Agents' Immigrant Lists) and persons on early migrant ships. The majority of the ships in these records sailed from British ports to Sydney. However, a few went to Newcastle and to Moreton Bay (Brisbane), which was part of New South Wales until 1859. A few ships sailed from Hamburg, Madras and New York.

## 12.7  Emigration to Canada

A high proportion of the emigrants from the West Country were nonconformists, particularly Bible Christians. This movement was founded in 1815 by James Thorne and William O'Bryan at Lake Farm in Shebbear parish in 1815, and its heartland lay in north-west Devon and north-east Cornwall. In 1831 there were sufficient numbers of Bible Christians in Canada for the movement to send two preachers to minister to them. Early censuses of Prince Edward Island and Ontario confirm that large numbers of Bible Christians were living in places like Port Hope and Charlottetown, and that they had originated from the West Country.

The early 1830s saw a surge of English emigration, bringing 5,600 West Country emigrants to Quebec. Significant though these numbers were, they pale in comparison to the 20,000 who arrived during the 1845–54 period. Plymouth remained the port of choice for emigration to central Canada through the 1820s and 1830s, but some quite small West Country havens, such as Padstow and Falmouth, contributed about a quarter of the numbers from 1830 to 1834. The small ports accounted for half the movement in the late 1840s and for about a quarter of it in the early 1850s, when Bideford finally assumed some minor significance in the Quebec traffic.

West Country emigrants were instrumental in forming the largest concentration of English immigrants in Upper Canada by the mid-nineteenth century, in York, Ontario and Durham counties, along the western half of the Lake Ontario shore between Port Hope and Toronto. In this area more than 30 per cent of the foreign-born population was English, and nine municipalities contained more than 1,000 natives of England in 1852; only Brantford Township and four of the five cities (Toronto, Kingston, Hamilton, and London) were home to as many. The English concentration was most notable in Darlington (foreign-born 56 per cent English), Whitby (47 per cent), Hope (41 per cent) and Clarke (34 per cent). These townships contained an overflow of the Yorkshire concentration further west but they were the heartland of the Devon and Cornwall settlers from 1830 onwards.

By the 1850s increasing numbers of West Country settlers were also locating to the north in Mariposa Township and in the Canada Company's Huron tract, where a settlement had been formed contemporaneously with Darlington's. The first settler located near the site of Exeter (named after the Devon city) in 1831 and returned to England to encourage his friends to follow; however, most came only in the late 1840s and 1850s.

### 12.7.1 Digging deeper

Canadian censuses are available online on the Ancestry website, starting with the 1851 Census of Canada East, Canada West, New Brunswick and Nova Scotia, followed by 1881, 1901 and then a 1916 Census of Manitoba, Saskatchewan and Alberta. The censuses provide place of birth, although sometimes only the country of birth, with no specific location given.

Harrison's *The Home Children* contains personal stories of more than a hundred children who were sent from Britain. The National Archives of Canada website features a database, prepared from ships' passenger lists, of about 100,000 children sent to Canada between 1869 and the 1930s. The Bristol Emigration Society started to send children to Canada in 1885. Taken from children's homes, industrial schools and reformatories, the children were placed through the Immigration Agent at St John, New Brunswick, with a few going to Marchmont Homes in Belleville, Ontario. Others were placed through the Women's Protective Society in Montreal.

Park Row Certified Industrial School used this society to send their children to Canada, as did the Industrial School of Bristol, although children of the latter establishment were placed in the Annapolis Valley area of Nova Scotia. Many of the children came from the local Unions. The Society continued to send children to Canada until 1906, by which time more than 300 children had been placed in New Brunswick, Nova Scotia, Quebec and Ontario.

Many Canadian passenger lists from 1865 to 1935 have been made available on the Ancestry website.

### 12.7.2 Hidden treasures

The Bristol Home Children website holds further information and includes a list of names of 1,200 children from Bristol who emigrated to Canada, with other details about the individuals, where known.

The Newfoundland Grand Banks website holds genealogical and historical data for the province of Newfoundland and Labrador, including births, marriages and deaths, gazetteers, trade directories, passenger lists, newspapers, photo albums and much more.

The North Devon Exodus Database of Surnames, under the auspices of the Bideford and District Community Archive, provides a list of individuals who emigrated from the north of Devon, naming their home parish and settlement place, with the vast majority of references relating to Canadian settlement.

An excellent resource for emigrants to Canada is provided by Marjorie P. Kohli, Waterloo, Ontario on the University of Waterloo Retirees Association website.

# BIBLIOGRAPHY

## Chapter Two

### Publications

Mee, Arthur, *The King's England: Devon*, Hodder & Stoughton Ltd, 1965

Mee, Arthur, *The King's England: Gloucestershire*, Hodder & Stoughton Ltd, 1966

Society for the Diffusion of Useful Knowledge, *The Market Towns of Devon in the early 19th century*, Old Towns Books & Maps, 2008

## Chapter Three

### Publications

Census of Great Britain, 1801, Abstract of the answers and returns made pursuant to an Act, passed in the forty-first year of His Majesty King George III. intituled 'An act for taking an account of the population of Great Britain, and the increase or diminution thereof'. Enumeration. Part I. England and Wales. Part II. Scotland BPP 1801–02 VI (9) 11

Chapman, Colin R., *Pre-1841 Censuses & Population Listings in the British Isles*, 4th edition, Lochin Publishing, 1994

Flower, Fred, *Somerset Coalmining Life – A miner's memories*, Millstream Books, 1990

Gibson, J.S.W. and Medlycott, M.T., *Local Census Listings 1522–1930*, 2nd edition, Birmingham, FFHS, 1994

Humphery-Smith, C.R., *The Phillimore Atlas & Index of Parish registers: England, Wales & Scotland*, Phillimore, 1995

Kain, Roger J.P. and Prince, Hugh C., *Tithe Surveys for Historians*, Phillimore, 2000

### Websites

www.digital-documents.co.uk/archi/placename.htm – Archaeology UK Place Name Search

www.gazetteer.co.uk – The Association of British Counties Gazetteer of British Place Names

www.histpop.org – Histpop – The Online Historical Population Reports Website

www.ordnancesurvey.co.uk/oswebsite/freefun/didyouknow – Ordnance Survey Place Names Gazetteer

www.visionofbritain.org.uk – A Vision of Britain Through Time – Great Britain Historical GIS Project

www.cassinimaps.co.uk – Cassini Maps

http://freepages.genealogy.rootsweb.ancestry.com/~genmaps – Genmaps, online images of maps from their beginnings to the twentieth century

www.oldmaps.co.uk – Old Maps

www.geograph.co.uk – Geograph Britain and Ireland, geographically representative photographs

maps.google.com/help/maps/streetview/ – Google Maps with Street View

www.one-place-studies.org – One Place Studies website

## Chapter Four

### Turnpikes

### Publications

Jenkinson, T. and Taylor, P., *The Toll-houses of South Devon*, Polystar Press, 2009

Jenkinson, T. and Taylor, P., *The Toll-houses of North Devon*, Polystar Press, 2010

Phillips D., *The great road to Bath*, Countryside Books, 1983

Taylor, P., *The Toll-houses of Cornwall*, The Federation of Old Cornwall Societies, 2001

Wright, G.N., *Turnpike roads*, Shire Publications, 1992

### Railways

### Publications

Atterbury, Paul, *Branch Line Britain*, David & Charles, 2005

Drummond, Di, *Tracing Your Railway Ancestors* Pen & Sword Books Ltd, 2010

Harris, Helen, *Devon's Railways*, Bossiney Books, 2008

Herring, Peter, *Yesterday's Railways*, David & Charles, 2004

Maggs, Colin G., *The GWR Bristol to Bath Line*, Sutton, 2001

Nock, O.S., *Historic Railway Disasters*, 2nd edition, Ian Allan, 1980

Richards, Tom, *Was Your Grandfather a Railwayman? – A directory of railway archive sources for family historians*, 4th edition, FFHS, 2002

Thomas, David St John, *A Regional History of the Railways of Great Britain, Volume 1: The West Country*, 6th edition, 1988, David & Charles, Newton Abbot


### *Inland waterways*

### Publications

Booker, F., *The Industrial Archaeology of the Tamar Valley*, David & Charles, 1967

Burton, Anthony and Pratt, Derek, *The Anatomy of Canals: The Early Years*, Tempus Publishing, 2001

Burton, Anthony and Pratt, Derek, *The Anatomy of Canals: Mania Years*, Tempus Publishing, 2002

Burton, Anthony and Pratt, Derek, *The Anatomy of Canals: Decline and Renewal*, Tempus Publishing, 2003

Cary, John, *New Itinerary*, 1798

Clew, Kenneth R., *The Exeter Canal*, Phillimore, 1984

Corble, Nick, *Britain's Canals: A Handbook*, Amberley, 2010

Corble, Nick, *James Brindley: The First Canal Builder*, Tempus Publishing, 2005

Hadfield, Charles, *The Canals of South West England*, David & Charles, 1967

Jackman, W.T., *The Development of Transportation in Modern England*, Cambridge University Press, 1916

Norway, Arthur H., *Highways & Byways in Devon & Cornwall*, Macmillan, 1897

Popplewell, Lawrence, *The Railways, Canal and Mines of Looe and Liskeard*, Oakwood Press, 1977

Wilkes, Sue, *Tracing Your Canal Ancestors*, Pen & Sword Books Ltd, 2011


### Websites

www.turnpikes.org.uk – Turnpike roads in England

www.nrm.org.uk – National Railway Museum

www.railwaysarchive.co.uk – Railways Archive

http://www2.warwick.ac.uk/services/library/mrc/explorefurther/subject_guides/family_history/ – University of Warwick's Modern Record Centre – Trade Union records

www.railwayancestors.org.uk – Railways Ancestors Family History Society www.railwaysarchive.co.uk – Railways Archive

www.spartacus.schoolnet.co.uk/railways.htm – Railways in the Nineteenth Century

www.postcardcollecting.co.uk – Reflections of a Bygone Age, postcards and books on Yesterday's counties

www.canalmaps.net – Canal Maps Archive website

## Chapter Five

### Publications

Barber, Chips, *The Story of Dartmoor Prison*, Obelisk Publications, 2010

Cockburn, J., *A History of English Assizes, 1558–1714*, Cambridge, 1972

Dell, Simon, *Mutiny on the Moor*, Forest Publishing, 2006

Dell, Simon, *Bicentenary of Dartmoor Prison*, The Dartmoor Company, 2009

England, Mike and Handley, Phil (eds, *Bodmin 1901–2000: A Century of Memories*, MPG Books, 2000

Gibson, J., *Poll books c1696–1872*, 3rd edition, FFHS, 1994

Gibson, J. and Rogers, C., *Electoral Registers since 1832*, FFHS, 1989

Hawkings , David, *Criminal Ancestors: A Guide to Historical Criminal Records in England and Wales*, Sutton, 1992

Herber, Mark, *Ancestral Trails: The Complete Guide to British Genealogy and Family History*, Sutton, 2004

Howard, John, *The State of the Prisons*, 1777

James, Trevor, *'There's One Away': Escapes from Dartmoor Prison*, Orchard Publications, 1999

James, Trevor, *About Dartmoor Prison*, Orchard Publications, 2001

James, Trevor, *About Princetown*, Orchard Publications, 2002

Joy, Ron, *Dartmoor Prison – A Complete Illustrated History, Volume One: The War Prison 1809–1816*, Halsgrove, 2002

Joy, Ron, *Dartmoor Prison – A Complete Illustrated History, Volume Two: The Convict Prison 1850–present day*, Halsgrove, 2002

Keith-Lucas, B., *English Local Government in the Nineteenth and Twentieth Centuries*, 1977

Landau, N., *The Justices of the Peace 1679–1760*, Berkeley, 1984

Marston, Edward, *Prison: Five hundred years of life behind bars*, TNA, 2009

Stanbrook, Elizabeth, *Dartmoor's War Prison and Church 1805–1817*, Quay Publications, 2002

Wade, Stephen, *Tracing your Criminal Ancestors*, Pen & Sword Books Ltd, 2009

Webb, S. and B., *The Parish and the County*, 1906

Webb, S. and B., *The Manor and the Borough*, 1908

## Websites

www.duchyofcornwall.org – Duchy of Cornwall website

www.dartmoor-prison.co.uk – Dartmoor Prison Museum and Visitor Centre

http://freepages.genealogy.rootsweb.ancestry.com/~linkinhorne/LKol lbooks.htm – Cornish poll books online www.britishnewspaper archive.co.uk – the British Newspaper Archive

www.oldbaileyonline.org – proceedings of the Old Bailey, 1674–1913

http://www.slq.qld.gov.au/info/fh/convicts – Convict transportation registers database (1787–1867) – State Library of Queensland

## Chapter Six

### Publications

Adolph, Anthony, *Tracing Your Family History*, Collins, 2008 (with particular reference to pp. 204–6)

Clowes, W.L., *The Royal Navy*, Chatham Publishing, 1987

Duffy, Michael, et al. (eds), *The New Maritime History of Devon*, two volumes, Conway Maritime Press, 1992

Firth, Sir C. and Davies, G., *The Regimental History of Cromwell's Army*, Clarendon Press, 1940

Fowler, Simon, *Tracing Your Army Ancestors*, Pen & Sword Books Ltd, 2006

Fowler, Simon, *Tracing Your Naval Ancestors*, Pen & Sword Books Ltd, 2011

Gibson, J. and Dell, A., *Tudor and Stuart muster rolls, a directory of holdings in the British Isles*, FFHS, 1991

Gray, Todd, *Early-Stuart Mariners and Shipping – The Maritime Surveys of Devon and Cornwall (1619–1635)*, Devon and Cornwall Record Society, 1990

Guthrig, Sylvia, *From Plymouth Dock to Devonport*, Devon Family History Society, 2007

Millard, V.F.L., *Ships of Devon and Cornwall 1652–1942*, Kenilworth Nautical Publishing Co., 1942

Peacock, E., *The Army Lists of the Roundheads and Cavaliers*, Chatto & Windus, 1874

Pye, Andrew and Woodward, Freddy, *The Historic Defences of Plymouth*, Exeter Archaeology, 1996

Rodger, N.A.M., *Naval Records for Genealogists*, HMSO, 1998

*Ships' Crew Lists: A Handlist of Records in the Devon Record Office*, 1987

Spencer, William, *Records of the Militia and Volunteer Forces*, PRO Publications, 1997

Spencer, William, *Family History in the Wars*, National Archives, 2007

**Websites**
www.cyber-heritage.co.uk – Cyber Heritage website
www.plymouthnavalmuseum.com – Plymouth Naval Museum
www.fleetairarm.com – Fleet Air Arm Museum, Yeovilton
www.rmg.co.uk – National Maritime Museum
www.nmmc.co.uk – National Maritime Museum, Cornwall
www.army.mod.uk – British Army website
www.london-gazette.co.uk – London Gazette
www.cwgc.org – Commonwealth War Graves Commission website
www.iwm.org.uk – Imperial War Museum
www.nam.ac.uk – National Army Museum
http://www.armymuseums.org.uk/trust.htm – Army Museums Ogilvy
  Trust

**Chapter Seven**

*Seafaring*

**Publications**
Aflalo, F.G., *The Sea-fishing Industry of England and Wales*, Edward
  Stanford, 1904
Corin, John, *Provident and the story of the Brixham Smacks*, Tops'l Books,
  1980
Dickinson, Michael G., *A Living from the Sea*, Devon Books, 1987
Ellis, Sheila, *Down a Cobbled Street: The Story of Clovelly*, Badger Books
  Ltd, 1987
Hippisley Coxe, Antony D., *A book about Smuggling in the West Country
  1700–1850*, Tabb House, 1984
Kain, Roger and Ravenhill, William (eds), *Historical Atlas of South-West
  England*, University of Exeter Press, 1999
Lenton, Stewart, *Fishing Boats and Ports of Cornwall*, Channel View
  Publishing, 2006
MacInnes, C.M., *Bristol and the Slave Trade*, Bristol Branch of the
  Historical Association, 1968
Minchinton, W.E., *The Port of Bristol in the Eighteenth Century*, Bristol
  Branch of the Historical Association, 1962
Shore, H.N., *Smuggling Days and Smuggling Ways*, Philip Allan & Co.
  Ltd, 1929 reprint
Smith, Graham, *Something to Declare*, London, 1980
Starkey, David J., *British Privateering Enterprise in the Eighteenth Century*,
  University of Exeter Press, 1990
Torbay Borough Council, *The Fishing Industry in Brixham*, The Council,
  1970

## Websites

www.devonmuseums.net/North-Devon-Maritime-Museum/Devon-Museums – North Devon Maritime Museum

www.smuggling.co.uk – Smugglers' Britain website

www.mariners-l.co.uk/UKFishermen.html – the website of the Mariners Mailing list

www.devonheritage.org – Devon Heritage website

www.smuggling.co.uk/ebooks/rattenbury.html – *Memoirs of a Smuggler,* Jack Rattenbury

## *Agriculture*

### Publications

Brown, Jonathan, *Tracing Your Rural Ancestors,* Pen & Sword Books Ltd, 2011

Hall, Stephen J.G. and Clutton-Brock, Juliet, *Two Hundred Years of British Farm Livestock,* British Museum [Natural History], 1989

Overton, Mark, *Agricultural Revolution in England: The Transformation of the Agrarian Economy 1500–1850,* Cambridge University Press, 1996

Thirsk, J. (ed.), *The Agrarian History of England and Wales,* Cambridge University Press: vol. IV, 1967; vol. V, 1985; vol. VI, 1989

Turner, M.E., Beckett, J.V. and Afton, B., *Farm Production in England 1700–1914,* Oxford University Press, 2001

Williamson, Tom, *The Transformation of Rural England: Farming and the Landscape, 1700–1870,* Exeter University Press, 2002

### Websites

www.reading.ac.uk/merl – Museum of Rural Life – Reading

www.foda.org.uk – Friends of Devon's Archives

http://privatewww.essex.ac.uk/~alan/family/N-Money.html – Relative Values of Sums of Money, Source: Department of Employment and Productivity, 1981

## *Mining*

### Publications

Aiken, S.R., *West Devon Mining: the influence of mining on the parish of Tavistock in the 19th century,* 1964

Barton, D.B., *A Guide to the Mines of West Cornwall,* D. Bradford Barton, 1963

Barton, D.B., *A History of Tin Mining and Smelting in Cornwall,* Cornwall Books, 1989

Bawden, M., 'Mines and mining in the Tavistock district [1810–1901]', Trans. Dev. Assoc. 46, 1914

Cornish, Joseph H., The History and Genealogy of the Cornish Families in America, Higginson Book Company, 2003

Greeves, Tom, Tin Mines and Tin Miners: A Photographic Record, Devon Books, 1986

Jenkin, Kenneth Hamilton, The Cornish Miner: an account of his life above and underground from early times, George Allen & Unwin, 1927: three editions, including 3rd edition, 1962 (reprinted by David & Charles, Newton Abbot, 1972; reprinted in facsimile with an introduction by John H. Trounson, Launceston: West Country, 2004)

Jenkin, Kenneth Hamilton, Mines and Miners of Cornwall, in 16 volumes, vols 1–14 originally published by the Truro Bookshop, 1961 onwards and reprinted by various organizations

Mayers, Lynne, Bal Maidens: Women and Girls of the Cornwall and Devon Mines, 2nd edition, Blaize Bailey Books, 2008

Newman, Phil, The Dartmoor Tin Industry – A Field Guide, Chercombe Press, 1998

Patrick, Amber, Morwellham Quay: a history: a Tamar Valley mining quay 1140–1900, Morwellham Quay Museum, 1990

Phillips, M.C., 'Revd John Jago and his Survey of Tavistock of 1784; Demographic Changes 1741–1871 and their Association with Mining Developments', in Gray, T. (ed.), Devon Documents, Devon & Cornwall Notes & Queries, Special Issue, 1996

Stanier, Peter, Mines of Cornwall and Devon: an historic photographic record, Twelveheads Press, 1998

**Websites**

www.bbc.co.uk/nationonfilm/location/south-west – BBC Nation on Film South West Region, filled with clips on mining

www.cornwallinfocus.co.uk/history/mindbase.php – Mining in Cornwall database

www.cmhrc.co.uk – Coal Mining History Resource Centre

www.cornwallinfocus.co.uk – Cornwall in Focus

www.balmaiden.co.uk – Bal Maidens of Cornwall and Devon

*Lace-making*

**Publications**

Coxhead, J.R.W. The Romance of the Wool, Lace and Pottery Trades in Honiton, 8th edition, P.H. Thrower, 1968

Inder, P.M., *Honiton Lace*, Exeter Museums Publication No. 55, 1979

Moody, A. Penderel, *Devon Pillow Lace: Its History and How to Make It*, Cassell & Co. Ltd, 1908

Toomer, Heather, *Lace: A guide to identification of old lace types and techniques*, Batsford, 1989

Whittaker, A.L., 'Honiton lace', *Devon Life*, vol. 4, no. 29, 1968, pp.17–20

Yallop, H.J., *The History of the Honiton Lace Industry*, University of Exeter, 1992

**Websites**

www.bbc.co.uk/devon/content/articles/2007/06/25/honiton_lace_arc hive_video_feature.shtml – video demonstrating the art of lace making

www.honitonmuseum.co.uk – Honiton Museum

www.devonfhs.org.uk/CD050.htm – Facsimile of Mrs Treadwin's book, *Antique Point and Honiton Lace*, 1873

www.devonfhs.org.uk/CD049.htm – Facsimile of A. Penderel Moody's book, *Devon Pillow Lace: Its History and How to Make It*, 1908

## Cider production

**Websites**

www.sheppyscider.com – Sheppy's Cider

www.ciderbrandy.co.uk – Somerset distillery

www.legendarydartmoor.co.uk/cider_moor.htm – Legendary Dartmoor – The Devil's Brew

## Tourism

**Websites**

www.edenproject.com – Eden Project

## General

**Publications**

Hurley, Beryl, (ed.), *The Book of Trades: Or Library of Useful Arts*, Wiltshire Family History Society: vol. 1, 1991; vol. 2, 1992; vol. 3, 1994

Waters, Colin, *Dictionary of Old Trades, Titles and Occupations*, 2nd edition, Countryside Books, 2002

## Chapter Eight

### Publications

Bell, James, *A New and Comprehensive Gazetteer of England and Wales*, 1834

Collins, L. (ed.), *Marriage Licences: abstracts and indexes in the library of the Society of Genealogists*, 2nd edition, SoG, 1983

Gibbens, L., *Basic Facts About Using Death and Burial Records for Family Historians*, FFHS, 1999

Gibson, J.S.W., *Bishops' Transcripts and marriage licences, bonds and allegations: a guide to their location and indexes*, 2nd edition, FFHS, 1985

Humphery-Smith, C.R., *The Phillimore Atlas & Index of Parish registers: England, Wales & Scotland*, Phillimore, 1995

Litton, P., *Basic Facts About Using Baptism Records for Family Historians*, FFHS, 1996

Litton, P., *Basic Facts About Using Marriage Records for Family Historians*, FFHS, 1996

### Websites

www.onlineparishclerks.org.uk – Online Parish Clerks

www.westcountrygenealogy.com – West Country genealogy website

## Chapter Nine

### Publications

Brockett, Allan A., *Nonconformity in Exeter 1650–1875*, Manchester University Press, 1962

Matthews, A. G., *Calamy Revised*, Clarendon Press, 1934

Mullett, M. *Sources for the History of English Nonconformity 1660-1830*, BRA, 1991

*My Ancestors were …: How Can I Find Out More About Them?*, available for various denominations, published by the Society of Genealogists

*Original Records of Early Nonconformity under Persecution and Indulgence*, 3 volumes, transcribed by Professor G. Lyon Turner, published by T. Fisher Unwin between 1911 and 1914

Pollock, John, *John Wesley 1703-1791*, Hodder and Stoughton, 1989

Short, Samuel. 'The diary (1705–1726) of Rev. Samuel Short, dissenting minister at Uffculme, Devon', *Devon & Cornwall Notes & Queries*, vol. 23 (1947–1949)

Steel, D. J., *Sources for Nonconformist genealogy and family history*, Phillimore, 1973

Steel, D. J., *Sources for Roman Catholic and Jewish genealogy and family history*, Phillimore, 1974

Stell, C., *Nonconformist Chapels and Meeting Houses in South-West England*, RCHME, 1991

**Websites**

www.hct.org.uk – Historic Chapels Trust (HCT)

www.spreadthetruth.co.uk/Articles/wesley.html – The Wesleys in Cornwall – Introduction

www.lamc.org.uk/wesleycottage – Wesley Cottage, Trewint, near Altarnun

www.newroombristol.org.uk – New Room, Bristol, with links to the electronic library catalogue

www.quaker.org.uk – Quakers website

www.urc.org.uk – United Reform Church History Society Library

www.bmdregisters.co.uk – BMD Registers

www.bristol.gov.uk/page/handlist-parish-registers-non-conformist-registers-and-bishops-transcripts – Bristol City Council, hand list of parish registers

www.southpethertoninformation.org.uk/NCR%20SP%20Wesleyan.pdf – South Petherton information website

www.jewishgen.org – Jewish genealogy website

www.jewishgen.org/JCR-UK/susser/susserpublications.htm – Susser Archive contents, Jewish genealogy website

www.plymouth.gov.uk/textonly/registerotherplacesworship – Plymouth City Council, list of other places of worship

www.dwlib.co.uk - Dr Williams's Library

## Chapter Ten

### Publications

Bovett, Robert, *Historical Notes on Devon Schools*, Devon County Council, 1989

Chapman, C. R. *The Growth of British Education and its Records*, Lochin Publishing, 1995

Horn, Pamela, *The Victorian and Edwardian schoolchild*, Sutton, 1989

May, Trevor, *The Victorian Schoolroom*, Shire, 1994

Morton, Ann, *Education and the State from 1833*, PRO Publications, 1997

Richardson, J. *The Local Historian's Encyclopaedia*, 2nd edition, Historical Publications, 2003

Riden, P., *Record sources for local history*, Batsford, 1987

Sellman, Roger R., *Devon Village Schools in the nineteenth century*, David & Charles, 1967

**Websites**

www.dwlib.co.uk – Dr Williams's Library

www.victoriacountyhistory.ac.uk – Victoria County History website

www.plymouthdata.info/Schools.htm – History of Plymouth's schools and other educational establishments

www.bristolinformation.co.uk/schools – Bristol Information website, Schools section

## Chapter Eleven

**Publications**

Briers, Richard, *English Country Churches*, PRC, 1995

Brooks, Pamela, *How to research local history*, 2nd edition, How to Books Ltd, 2008

*The Compleat Parish Officer*, Wiltshire Family History Society – reprint of 1734 edition setting out the duties of various parish officers and the law as it related to them

*Family and Local History Handbook*, various years, published by Robert Blatchford

Fowler, Simon, *Workhouses*, TNA, 2009

Gibson, J., Rogers, C. and Webb, C., *Poor Law Union Records Vol.1 – South East England and East Anglia*, 2nd edition, FFHS, 1997

Gibson, J. and Rogers, C., *Poor Law Union Records Vol.2 – The Midlands and Northern England*, FFHS, 1993

Gibson, J. and Rogers, C., *Poor Law Union Records Vol. 3 – South-West England, The Marches and Wales*, FFHS, 1993

Gibson, J. and Churchill, E., *Probate Jurisdictions, Where to Look for Wills*, FFHS, 2002

Grannum, Karen and Taylor, Nigel, *Wills and Probate Records*, National Archives, 2009

Herber, Mark, *Ancestral Trails: The Complete Guide to British Genealogy and Family History*, Sutton, 2004 – excellent chapters on Parish and Town Records, Wills and Administrations

Higginbotham, Peter, *Life in a Victorian Workhouse*, Pitkin Unichrome Ltd, 2011

Higginbotham, Peter, *The Workhouse Encyclopedia*, History Press Ltd, 2012

Higginbotham, Peter, *Voices from the Workhouse*, forthcoming

Higginbotham, Peter, *A Grim Almanac of the Workhouse*, forthcoming

Jewer, A.J., *Marriage Allegation Bonds of the Bishops of Bath and Wells*, 1909

McLaughlin, Eve, *Annals of the Poor*, FFHS, 1987

May, Trevor, *The Victorian Workhouse*, Shire Publications Ltd, 1997

Philp, Tony, *A Social History of Bodmin Union Workhouse*, Bodmin Town Museum, 2005

Pope, Stephen, *Gressenhall Farm and Workhouse: A history of the buildings and the people who lived in them*, Poppyland Publishing, 2006

Raymond, S., *Devon; a genealogical biography; vol. 1 Genealogical sources, vol. 2 Devon family histories and pedigrees*, FFHS, 2nd edition, 1994

Raymond, S., *Cornwall: A Genealogical Bibliography*, 2nd edition, S.A. and M.J. Raymond, 1994

Salter, Mike, *The Old Parish Churches of Devon*, Folly Publications, 1999

Salter, Mike, *The Old Parish Churches of Cornwall*, Folly Publications, 1999

Webb, C.C., *A Guide to Genealogical Sources at the Borthwick Institute of Historical Research*, 3rd edition, York University, 1996

Wild, Trevor, *Village England: A Social History of the Countryside*, I.B. Taurus, 2004

Yorke, Trevor, *Tracing the history of villages*, Countryside Books, 2001

**Websites**

www.workhouses.org.uk – The Workhouse website

http://www.nationaltrust.org.uk/workhouse-southwell/ – The Workhouse at Southwell

www.museums.norfolk.gov.uk – Gressenhall Farm and Workhouse

www.riponmuseums.co.uk – The Workhouse Museum, Ripon

www.sog.org.uk – Society of Genealogists

www.worldburialindex.com – World Burial Index

www.deceasedonline.co.uk – Deceased Online

www.york.ac.uk/library/borthwick – Borthwick Institute of Historical Research

http://genuki.cs.ncl.ac.uk/DEV/DevonWillsProject – Devon Wills Project

http://pub.exeter.gov.uk/asp/bereavement/ – Alphabetical index cards images, Exeter cemeteries

www.arnosvale.org.uk – Arnos Vale Cemetery, Bristol

http://members.cornwallfhs.com/research/research_locations_index.search.php?q_location=cemetery&submit=Search – Cornwall FHS, filmed and transcribed cemetery registers

http://www.devon.gov.uk/fs29_-_researching_devon_workhouses_in_the_westcountry_stu_.pdf – Devon Libraries – researching Devon workhouses in the Westcountry Studies Library

http://www1.somerset.gov.uk/archives/Leaflets/PoorLaw.pdf – Somerset Archive and Record Service, Poor Law information leaflet

## Chapter Twelve

### Publications

Bromell, A., *Tracing Family History in New Zealand*, Government Printing Office Publishing, 1988

Bromell, A., *They Came in Waves; conference proceedings*, New Zealand Society of Genealogists, 2003

Hall, Nick Vine, *Tracing Your Family History in Australia*, Rigby, 1994

Harrison, P., *The home children*, 3rd edition, Watson & Dwyer Publishing, 1979

Hawkings, David, *Bound for Australia*, Phillimore, 1987

Hey, David, *The Oxford guide to family history*, OUP, 1993

Kershaw, Roger, *Emigrants and Expats: A guide to sources on UK emigration and residents overseas*, PRO, 2002

Peake, Andrew, *National Register of Shipping Arrivals, Australia and New Zealand*, 3rd edition, AFFHO, 1992

### Websites

http://emigrated.bafhs.org.uk – Bristol Home Children website

www.collectionscanada.gc.ca – National Archives of Canada

http://ngb.chebucto.org/ – Newfoundland Grand Banks website, genealogical and historical data for the Province of Newfoundland and Labrador

www.bathspa.ac.uk/schools/humanities-and-cultural-industries/irish-studies/research-projects/shovelling-out-paupers.pdf – Graham Davis's article 'Shovelling out paupers?': Emigration from Ireland and the South-West of England, 1815–1850

www.collectionscanada.gc.ca/databases/home-children – Library and Archives Canada website, Home Children (1869–1930)

http://genuki.cs.ncl.ac.uk/DEV/DevonMisc/NDevonExodusListing.html – North Devon Exodus Database of Surnames

www.theshipslist.com/ships/passengerlists/index.htm – The Ships List

www.emigrants.net.au – an online aid for those seeking emigrant passenger lists

www.slq.qld.gov.au/info/fh/immigration – State Library of Queensland, thorough research guide to immigration records held in relation to various Australian states

www.naa.gov.au – National Archives of Australia

http://jubilation.uwaterloo.ca/~marj/genealogy/thevoyage.html – Immigration to Canada in the nineteenth century, provided by Marjorie P. Kohli, Waterloo, Ontario http://cornwall-opc.org/Resc/emigration_nz.php – Cornwall OPC website with emigration links relating to New Zealand

http://cornwall-opc.org/Resc/emigration_australia.php – Cornwall OPC website with emigration links relating to Australia

www.archives.govt.nz – Archives New Zealand website

www.genealogy.org.nz – New Zealand Society of Genealogists

www.natlib.govt.nz/at – Alexander Turnbull Library in Wellington

isbndb.com/d/publisher/bab_microfilming.html – BAB Microfilming, Auckland, New Zealand

## Resources directory

### Archives, libraries and local studies centres

Bristol Record Office, B Bond Warehouse, Smeaton Road, Bristol, BS1 6XN
Tel: +44 (0) 117 922 4224
Email: bro@bristol.gov.uk
Website: www.bristol.gov.uk/page/records-and-archives

Somerset Heritage Centre, Brunel Way, Langford Mead, Norton Fitzwarren, Taunton, TA2 6SF
Tel: +44 (0) 1823 278805
Email: archives@somerset.gov.uk
Website: www.somerset.gov.uk/archives

Bath Record Office, Guildhall, High Street, Bath, BA1 5AW
Tel: +44 (0) 1225 477421
Email: archives@bathnes.gov.uk
Website: www.batharchives.co.uk

Devon Heritage Centre, Great Moor House, Bittern Road, Sowton, Exeter, Devon, EX2 7NL
Tel: +44 (0)1392 384253
Email: devrec@devon.gov.uk
Website: http://www.devon.gov.uk/record_office.htm

North Devon Record Office, Tuly Street, Barnstaple, EX32 7EJ
Tel: +44 (0)1271 388607/8
Email: ndevrec@devon.gov.uk
Website: http://www.devon.gov.uk/index/community/the_county/record_office/north_record_office.htm

Plymouth and West Devon Record Office, Community Services
Department, Unit 3, Clare Place, Plymouth, PL4 0JW
Tel: +44 (0) 1752 305940
Email: pwdro@plymouth.gov.uk
Website: http://www.plymouth.gov.uk/archives

Devon and Cornwall Record Society, Westcountry Studies Library, Great
Moor House, Bittern Road, Sowton, Exeter, Devon, EX2 7NL
Tel: +44 (0)1392 384253
Email: devrec@devon.gov.uk

Cornwall Record Office, County Hall, Truro, TR1 3AY
Tel: +44 (0) 1872 323127
Email: cro@cornwall.gov.uk
Website: www.cornwall.gov.uk/default.aspx?page=24656

Cornwall Studies Library, Alma Place, Redruth, TR15 2AT
Email: cornishstudies.library@cornwall.gov.uk
Website: www.chycor.co.uk/general/red-lib/

National Archives, Kew, Richmond, Surrey, TW9 4DU
Tel: +44 (0) 8876 3444
Website: www.nationalarchives.gov.uk

House of Lords Record Office, Parliamentary Archives, Houses of
Parliament, London, SW1A 0PW
Tel: +44 (0) 20 7219 3074
Email: archives@parliament.uk
Website: www.parliament.uk/archives

### Other useful organizations and resources

Bristol and Avon Family History Society, Research Room c/o Bristol
Record Office, B Bond Warehouse, Smeaton Road, Bristol, BS1 6XN
Email: secretary@bafhs.org.uk
Website: www.bafhs.org.uk/index.php

Weston-super-Mare and District Family History Society
Website: http://wsmfhs.org.uk

Somerset & Dorset Family History Society, PO Box 4502, Sherborne, DT9 6YL
Tel: +44 (0) 1935 389611
Email: sdfhs@btconnect.com
Website: www.sdfhs.org

Devon Family History Society, PO Box 9, Exeter, Devon, EX2 6YP
Tel: +44 (0) 1392 433212
Email: secretary@devonfhs.org.uk
Website: www.devonfhs.org.uk

Friends of Devon's Archives, c/o Devon Heritage Centre, Great Moor House, Bittern Road, Sowton, Exeter, EX2 7NL
Email: friends_info@foda.org.uk
Website: www.foda.org.uk

Cornwall Family History Society, 18 Lemon Street, Truro, Cornwall, TR1 2LS
Tel: +44 (0) 1872 264044
Email: secretary@cornwallfhs.com
Website: www.cornwallfhs.com

Federation of Family History Societies (FFHS), PO Box 8857, Lutterworth, LE17 9BJ
Tel: +44 (0) 1455 203133
Email: admin@ffhs.org.uk
Website: www.ffhs.org.uk

*General*

North Devon Maritime Museum, Odun House, Odun Road, Appledore, Devon, EX39 1PT
Tel: +44 (0) 1237 422064
Email: info@northdevonmaritimemuseum.co.uk
Website: www.northdevonmaritimemuseum.co.uk

National Maritime Museum, Discovery Quay, Falmouth, Cornwall, TR11 3QY
Tel: +44 (0) 1326 313388
Email: enquiries@nmmc.co.uk
Website: www.nmmc.co.uk

Imperial War Museum, Lambeth Road, London, SE1 6HZ
Tel: +44 (0)20 7416 5320
Email: mail@iwm.org.uk
Website: www.iwm.org.uk

Duke of Cornwall's Light Infantry Museum, The Keep, Bodmin, PL31 1EG
Tel: +44 (0) 1208 72810
Email: dclimus@lightinfantry.org
Website: www.britisharmedforces.org/li_pages/regiments/dcli/duke_museum.htm

Honiton Allhallows Museum, High Street, Honiton, EX14 1PG
Tel: +44 (0)1404 44966
Email: info@honitonmuseum.co.uk
Website: www.honitonmuseum.co.uk

The Workhouse, Upton Road, Southwell, NG25 0PT
Tel: +44 (0) 1636 817260
Email: theworkhouse@nationaltrust.org.uk
Website: www.nationaltrust.org/workhouse

Gressenhall Farm and Workhouse, Gressenhall, East Dereham, Norfolk, NR20 3DR
Tel: +44 (0) 1362 869263
Website: www.museums.norfolk.gov.uk

The Workhouse Museum, Allhallowgate, Ripon HG4 1LE
Tel: +44 (0) 1765 690799
Email: info@riponmuseums.co.uk
Website: www.riponmuseums.co.uk

Somerset Distillery, Somerset Cider & Brandy Co. Ltd, Pass Vale Farm, Burrow Hill, Kingsbury Episcopi, Somerset, TA12 5BU
Tel: +44 (0) 1460 240782
Email: apples@ciderbrandy.co.uk
Website: www.ciderbrandy.co.uk

United Reform Church History Society Library, Westminster College, Madingley Road, Cambridge, CM3 0AA
Tel: +44 (0) 1223 741300

Email: mt212@cam.ac.uk
Website: www.urc.org.uk

Borthwick Institute for Archives, University of York, Heslington, York, YO10 5DD
Tel: +44 (0) 1904 321166
Email: bihr500@york.ac.uk
Website: www.york.ac.uk/library/borthwick

Guildhall Library, Aldermanbury, London, EC2P 2EJ
Tel: +44 (0) 20 7332 1862
Email: manuscripts.guildhall@cityoflondon.gov.uk
Website: www.cityoflondon.gov.uk/guildhalllibrary

Society of Genealogists, 14 Charterhouse Buildings, Goswell Road, London, EC1M 7BA
Tel: +44 (0) 20 7251 8799
Email: genealogy@sog.org.uk
Website: www.sog.org.uk

Dr Williams's Library, 14 Gordon Square, London, WC1H 0AR
Tel: +44 (0) 20 7387 3727
Email: enquiries@dwlib.co.uk
Website: www.dwlib.co.uk

Library of Religious Society of Friends, Friends House, 173–177 Euston Road, London, NW1 2BJ
Tel: +44 (0) 20 7663 1000
Email: enquiries@quaker.org.uk
Website: www.quaker.org.uk/library

Lambeth Palace Library, London, SE1 7JU
Tel: +44 (0) 20 7898 1400
Email: archives@churchofengland.org
Website: www.lambethpalacelibrary.org

Archbishop of Canterbury's Faculty Office, 1 The Sanctuary, Westminster, London, SW1P 3JT
Tel: +44 (0) 20 7222 5381
Email: faculty.office@1thesanctuary.com
Website: www.facultyoffice.org.uk

### General web resources

www.findmypast.co.uk

www.ancestry.co.uk

www.familysearch.org – The Church of Jesus Christ of the Latter-day Saints

www.genuki.org.uk – provides a virtual reference library of genealogical information of particular relevance to the UK and Ireland. It is a non-commercial service, maintained by a charitable trust and a group of volunteers.

www.nationalarchives.gov.uk – The National Archives website

www.nationalarchives.gov.uk/a2a – Access to Archives, with references to sources in archives across the country

www.historicaldirectories.org – Historical Directories

http://neighbourhood.statistics.gov.uk/dissemination – Office for National Statistics: Neighbourhood statistics

www.british-history.ac.uk – British History Online, home of the Journal of the House of Commons and the House of Lords, plus much more

www.britishnewspaperarchive.co.uk – The British Newspaper Archive

# INDEX

Wells, 9–10
  bishops, 97–8
  Turnpike Trust, 34–5
  Wells Cathedral, 9–10
Wesley, Charles, 103, 113
Wesley, John, 103–4, 106, 111–14
West Cornwall Railway, 43
West Somerset Railway, 40, 86

Westbury on Trym, 8
Wheal Betsy, 13–14, 24, 83
White, Revd John, 143–4
wool trade, 7, 10
workhouse, 54, 131–2, 136, 138–40

Yealmbridge toll-house, 38

# Tracing Your Family History?

## Read Your Family HISTORY

### ESSENTIAL ADVICE FROM THE EXPERTS

**FREE COPY!**

*Your Family History* is the only magazine that is put together by expert genealogists. Our editorial team, led by Dr Nick Barratt, is passionate about family history, and our networks of specialists are here to give essential advice, helping readers to find their ancestors and solve those difficult questions.

In each issue we feature a **Beginner's Guide** covering the basics for those just getting started, a **How To ...** section to help you to dig deeper into your family tree and the opportunity to **Ask The Experts** about your tricky research problems. We also include a **Spotlight** on a different county each month and a **What's On** guide to the best family history courses and events, plus much more.

**Receive a free copy** of *Your Family History* magazine and gain essential advice and all the latest news. To request a free copy of a recent back issue, simply e-mail your name and address to marketing@your-familyhistory.com or call 01226 734302*.

*Your Family History* is in all good newsagents and also available on subscription for six or twelve issues. For more details on how to take out a subscription, call 01778 392013 or visit **www.your-familyhistory.co.uk**.

**Alternatively read issue 31 online completely free using this QR code**

*Free copy is restricted to one per household and available while stocks last.

## www.your-familyhistory.com